DAN FEIGELSON

RADICAL LISTENING

Reading and Writing Conferences to Reach All Students

SCHOLASTIC

For my friend Maurice Berger
(May 22, 1956–March 22, 2020),
a radical listener whose voice lives on

Acquisitions editor: Lois Bridges
Editorial director: Sarah Longhi
Development editor: Raymond Coutu
Senior editor: Shelley Griffin
Production editor: Danny Miller
Designer: Maria Lilja

Photos ©: cover top: Courtesy of Marvin Heiferman; cover bottom and throughout: Aleksei Derin/
Shutterstock; back cover: Courtesy of Mary Cybulski; 12, 33: FatCamera/Getty Images; 21, 90, 102: Ming
Yang Education, Shenzhen, China; 48: SDI Productions/Getty Images; 78: LumiNola/Getty Images; 83, 115:
Monkey Business Images/Shutterstock; 126: Lopolo/Shutterstock; 154: Courtesy of Dave Caleb; All other
photos courtesy of the author.

ISBN 978-1-338-80999-2

SCHOLASTIC and associated logos are trademarks and/or registered trademarks of Scholastic Inc.

1 2 3 4 5 6 7 8 9 10   40   31 30 29 28 27 26 25 24 23 22

Scholastic Inc., 557 Broadway, New York, NY 10012

Contents

ACKNOWLEDGMENTS

The best conversations are those that continue in your head after the other person leaves. Sometimes, it's what your conversation partner said that lingers. Other times, it's the way they listened.

I've had the good fortune to learn about listening from children, teachers, and administrators around the world. This book is the result—and hopefully the continuation—of those conversations. What follows is a woefully inadequate list of some of the individuals who have contributed to my thinking.

Several colleagues in the world of literacy instruction endured phone calls, texts, and emails at many points along the way. Carl Anderson was there on a near-daily basis with feedback, pushback, and a nifty book title. Old friends Ralph Fletcher and JoAnn Portalupi weighed in on early chapters with editorial and conceptual tips. Ellin Keene, Colleen Cruz, Kelly Gallagher, and Kathy Collins contributed illuminating perspectives. Besides composing a gorgeous foreword, several eye-opening conversations with Cornelius Minor informed and expanded my ideas about what it means to create equity and access for all children.

It is difficult to narrow down the list of teachers and administrators I've learned from and with over the years. Particularly provocative have been my ongoing dialogues with Courtney Al Moreno at the American Embassy School in New Delhi, India; Tiana Silvas from P.S. 59 and 277 in New York City; Franco Rodriguez from Shen Wai International School in Shenzhen, China; Ryan Scala at Springs School, East Hampton, NY; Jesse Meyer, Keith Stanulis, Jay Monson, and Don Drake at Hong Kong International School; Heather Onderick from Asociaciòn Escuelas Lincoln in Buenos Aires; Leilani Greene, also at Asociaciòn Escuelas Lincoln in Buenos Aires; Kimberly Fung and Tanja Galetti at Hong Kong Academy; Praxia Apostle, Paige Emerich, Su-Yen Chan, and Joel Llaban at International School of Kuala Lumpur; Katie Vis, Steve Vis, and Jessica Krueger at International School of Latvia; Robyn Ibrahim and Nargiza Azizova at Tashkent International School; Aybike Oğuz, Andrea Holck, and Maura Kelly from Robert College in Istanbul; Amy Richie, Maureen Ienuso, and Raquel Acedo-Rubio at Mt. Zaagkam School in Papua, Indonesia; Jude Griffith and Kerryl Howarth at the Australian International School of Singapore; Fiona Bullard, Amy Lee, and Chelsea Miolee at American International School of Guangzhou; Steve DiSalvo and Mariem Alchoum at Lavelle School in Staten Island; Adele Schroeter and my niece Sarah Feigelson at PS 59, Manhattan; Sonya Simpson at Satellite Middle School in Bed-Stuy, Brooklyn; Cheryl Tyler from PS 277 in the Bronx; Jorge Perdomo, Katrina Garcia, Lana Vogelle, and Tacia Maxwell from PS 1 in the Bronx; Margaret

Ruller from Hendrick Hudson School District in Westchester, New York; Ryan Bourke of Will Rogers Learning Community in Santa Monica, California; Katrina Theilmann at American School of Doha; Amanda Jacob from Taipei American School; Amanda Knight at the American Overseas School of Rome; and Alexa Schmid at International School of Kenya. In the course of writing, I conjured their classrooms and schools frequently. Thanks, too, to Sarah Cheng at Peak School in Hong Kong, Nira Naik from AES in New Delhi, Deborah Larsson and Caitlin Tomassi from Hendrick Hudson, and Anna Schlosser of the American School of The Hague for their contributions.

Countless sunset conversations with my brilliant friend Marvin Heiferman were critical in shaping this manuscript—and his eleventh-hour photography provided a stellar cover. My co-founder in the Russian Literature and Drinking Club, John Tintori, always informs my thinking about books and storytelling. The marvelous Mary Cybulski took time out from the world of film to take an author photo, which looks far better than I do in real life. Brother-from-another-mother David Konigsberg and the intrepid Peg Patterson kept track of my comings and goings and welcomed me home after many travels. Zoltan Sarda's irreverence and video-editing skills were invaluable as well.

It was Lois Bridges who initially invited me to write for Scholastic, and our dialogue throughout the beginning stages of writing informed and shaped my thinking in, yes, radical ways. Ray Coutu and Sarah Longhi provided erudite commentary throughout the process and were cheerleaders when I most needed them, in sickness and in health. Danny Miller and Maria Lilja took my typewritten words and designed a beautiful book

Much of what I know about listening comes from watching jazz musicians. As this book took shape, I was lucky to hear Jason Moran, Bill Frisell, Vijay Iyer, Linda May Han Oh, Tyshawn Sorey, Brian Blade, Cecile McLorin-Salvant, Sullivan Fortner, and Ron Miles perform in New York City. Each of these masters could have stolen the show with their virtuosic technique and vast musical knowledge, but instead held back and listened to one another. The resulting collaborations were greater and more beautiful than the sum of their parts.

My daughter Sonia is never afraid to question basic assumptions and is one of the best writers I know. She inspires everything I do, this book included. I am also indebted to Kiri Hogue for speaking truth even when it is uncomfortable. Continuing on the family front, a tip of the hat to Dr. Liz Feigelson, an amazing listener; and brother Jeremy, who always shows up when you need him.

This book would not have been possible without Suzy Stein. Her patience, intelligence, perspective, and sparkling eyes lit the way from early scribbles to final drafts. I send her gratitude, love, and all sorts of things that don't fit in book acknowledgments.

Finally, deepest thanks to the children I've conferred with in small and large schools throughout Africa, Asia, Europe, North America, and South America. They are the true teachers.

FOREWORD by CORNELIUS MINOR

Here, Dan Feigelson is clear about one thing: Listening to children matters. More than anything we do as educators, authentically seeing, hearing, and affirming kids matters. But we've all got so much to do. The world is too much. How do we find the time?

I don't have to tell you how intense things are in the world right now. You feel it. Those of us who love, live, and work with young people, we feel it many times over as it impacts the children around us.

But I'm not just talking about the challenges of being a COVID-era educator. So much about life in response to the virus was new to us, but the way that people have politicized the response, denied the impact of the virus, capitalized on misinformation, and neglected vulnerable communities... that ain't new.

I have spent my adult life in Brooklyn, but I was raised right outside of Atlanta by Black women who saw clearly and spoke truthfully...

Down South we say, "We seen this coming. We know what it is. We been knowing."

We saw the politicized response to Hurricane Katrina on the Gulf Coast. We watched those who denied the science of climate change. We tried to laugh away the nonsense theories and misinformation that has halted American democracy. We watched in disbelief as historically marginalized communities were vilified in discourse, and we gasped in horror as that discourse often resulted in violence against our Asian friends, our loved ones in the queer community, and our Jewish neighbors.

The last two decades have been a cascading prelude to this moment.

This moment does not deserve a sequel. It needs a reset. A reimagination. Something better can exist.

We know. We been knowing.

But here's the thing that I learned from my mother and all her sisters: Knowing means nothing if it is hoarded.

The first step to forging conditions better than the ones that we endure now is by sharing what we know about current conditions with those who will create better ones: the children.

This is conferring. This has been Dan's work. For a lifetime.

Our children do not build love, criticality, or a desire for justice if we do not share what we know about these things first.

Love, criticality, and a desire for justice do not spring out of the ether or out of a desire to simply be "nice" or "kind." They grow out of a careful study of the human condition and from thoughtful reflection about our relationship to it.

This is reading and writing. This has been Dan's work. For a lifetime.

The path to a better future for our children and for our world is not about the abstract notion of hope. Rather it is about the concrete notion of preparation. This is what Malcolm X meant when he theorized that "the future belongs to those who prepare for it today."

Dan has been preparing children. For a lifetime.

Here, he shares much of what he has learned on that journey. Dan understands that the most transformative and memorable moments in a classroom are not those when an educator is presenting to the whole class. They are the moments when an educator takes the time to see, to hear, and to teach an individual student.

The most transformative and memorable moments in a classroom are not those when an educator is presenting to the whole class. They are the moments when an educator takes the time to see, to hear, and to teach an individual student.

As our days become filled with professional demands that might pull us away from this vital work, Dan makes a case here for us to invest in it, and he shows us how to make the most of this sacred time.

Children can be powerful readers and thoughtful writers. But the future will demand more of them. They will need to be analytical, creative, and bold.

They will need to love fiercely, think critically, and put all of that to work as they sustain families and build communities. And they will have to do that while wielding the lessons learned from the past to illuminate the future.

This is big work. It is rooted in reading and writing—seeing the human condition and responding to it—and it all starts in a conference, at a desk, with a kid.

This kind of learning doesn't just transform a classroom. If our work is to build a reality that is better than the one that we share now, it might be the very learning that transforms our world.

Why Confer?

"Equity is hearing someone's voice about what they need and providing them with that."

—Christopher Emdin

This is a book on the art of conferring with individual children about their reading and writing. While conferences can provide opportunities to cover curriculum, help students meet year-end expectations, and target specific strengths and needs, these aren't the reasons kids remember them years later. For many, individual conferences are the first place in school where they feel heard and seen, maybe the first time an adult other than their parent is interested in what they have to say.

Reading and writing have always been a means to forge identity, to find our place in the world. Through reading we develop points of view and get a glimpse into possibilities beyond our experience. Writing often helps us clarify what we think and express it to others. "Books are a form of political action," suggests novelist Toni Morrison. "Books are knowledge. Books are reflection. Books change your mind."

It follows then that some percentage of time spent on literacy instruction should be consciously devoted to helping children develop their individual ways of knowing. Teaching with this objective in mind looks different from the teaching we do to cover predetermined content. The best way to support and develop individual thinking is to work one on one with a child, focusing on—and celebrating—her unique understandings. Exactly what we do in a conference.

There is often a tension between the standards teachers are told they must teach, and the strengths and needs of the individual children who walk into their classrooms. This disconnect shows up most glaringly in the disproportionate number of Black and Brown students failing in school compared to their White classmates—the so-called achievement gap. "But what if," writes Ibram X. Kendi (2019) "...these well-meaning efforts at closing the achievement gap have been opening the door to racist ideas?...What if we realized the best way to ensure an effective educational system is not by standardizing our curricula and tests but by standardizing the opportunities available to all students?"

It's probably unrealistic to expect standardized literacy curricula and tests to go away anytime soon—and of course there are common, specific things we want students to know and be able to do as readers and writers if they are to succeed in school and in life. As teachers, however, we have the power to balance important whole-class and small-group lessons with individual, one-on-one reading and writing conferences that honor individual student thinking.

Conferring can provide individual time in support of curriculum and standards, but, just as importantly, it can create a space where children feel their own ideas and experiences are the most important thing. "That's at the core of equity: understanding who your kids are and how to meet their needs," says Pedro Noguera (2016). "You are still focused on outcomes, but the path to get there may not be the same for each one."

Sometimes by prioritizing their individual thinking and experience, conferences can also help students connect to whole-class objectives.

Tiana Silvas, then a literacy coach at P.S. 277 in the South Bronx, tells of her experience with fourth grader Naima:

> "She was new to the school. In fact, 277 was her third elementary school, and she hadn't had good experiences at the other two. We had been studying nonfiction, using mentor texts from the unit of study books. Naima was not interested. She didn't want to learn how to do research or take notes, which were the big goals of the unit. She had a few laminated articles in her backpack, so when we sat down for a reading conference, I asked about them. At first, she didn't want to show me, and said 'These aren't for school.' I invited her to show me them when she was ready. Naima took me up on the offer, and it turned out they were about her older cousin, who'd been shot in a drug-related crossfire. This was obviously a lot more important to her than talking about note-taking skills. Once Naima saw it was okay to 'go off book'—that it was okay to talk about her life rather than the lesson—she got interested. I asked if she'd like to do some writing in her notebook about it, just sort of free-write—what happened, her feelings, her questions. It was the first time she'd gotten excited about anything in school, and it opened the door to understanding that writing could be personally meaningful."

> "What she ended up writing was a mix of questions about guns, feelings about how much she missed her cousin, and anger at the people who shot her—really strong, emotional stuff. We met again to talk about it all, and Naima decided she wanted to learn about how people got guns, what the laws were, and why people didn't do more to stop things like what happened to her cousin. Out of these conferences, she started doing some seriously rigorous reading and writing—looking at the Second Amendment, going over police reports from our neighborhood, reading and eventually writing editorials about gun control. Actually, the whole class got involved. Naima wasn't the only one who had been affected by gun violence."

The equity work here goes beyond the obvious. Yes, Naima was a Black student in a low-income neighborhood at a public school. Her conference and the teaching that grew out of it directly addressed an experience not likely to be shared by a White student of privilege. At the same time, Tiana's moves can be generalized beyond Naima's particular situation.

First, she listened and observed carefully before leaping in with teacher content (more on this later). Next, she validated her student's interests and needs over and above the planned curriculum and then taught a useful writing strategy (e.g., free-write to explore your topic). Finally, she helped Naima identify resources (Second Amendment, police reports, editorials) that spoke to her interests. What started as a reading conference in a nonfiction unit became an opportunity to use both reading and writing to support her desire to know. In the words of Gholdy Muhammad (2020), Tiana created an opportunity for her student "to shape (her) own ideas through acts of literacy." And in the end Naima was motivated to learn something about how to research a topic and take notes.

Children are quick to pick up on our beliefs about their abilities, and more often than not will rise—or sink—to meet that expectation.

If equity in teaching involves honoring individual differences while offering similar opportunities, the first step is to find the right entry point for every student. Tiana understood that before Naima would be open to learning, she needed to feel engaged. As Ellin Keene (2018) points out "...when we are engaged, we learn more, remember more, and reapply our understandings in new situations more effectively." It's important to remember, however, that engagement doesn't come from without.

A teacher needs to listen and observe, looking for the potential spark that may be ignited within an individual child. Approaching a conference as an opportunity to find that spark opens up new possibilities beyond the curriculum. It also requires coming in without preconceived assumptions about what a student can or can't do. Children are quick to pick up on our beliefs about their abilities, and more often than not will rise—or sink—to meet those expectations.

In this book, I offer practical advice on conducting individual conferences so children develop identities as readers and writers. There will be examples along the way, as well as step-by-step suggestions for how to listen to, honor, and extend student thinking. Though we'll also discuss strategies for connecting conferring work to curriculum goals, this book is meant as an invitation to prioritize what's inside the child in front of us.

When conferences become opportunities to find the spark in an individual child and focus on strengths—rather than on what she or he can't do—we move a little closer to equity.

CHAPTER ONE

On Listening

*"Some day I'm gonna call me up on the phone,
so when I answer, I can tell myself to shut up."*
—**Miles Davis**

Mr. Bratspies, my fifth-grade teacher, was the reason I became a teacher. Just out of college, he was definitely the coolest grown-up at Whittier School. I admired his bell-bottoms and groovy sideburns, how he seemed more tuned in than the other adults in the building. Especially in English class, we did more "creative" activities than the other fifth-grade rooms. I remember feeling I'd discovered some hidden secret as we analyzed the lyrics to Simon and Garfunkel's "Sounds of Silence."

One day in English class, Mr. Bratspies brought in several large photographs to inspire our writing. They were black and white, with street scenes—buildings at odd angles, city people going about their everyday activities. Our job was to pick one and do a quick-write, whatever came into our heads. I chose a picture of a little boy running across what looked like an apartment building rooftop, seemingly out of breath. He looked scared. One idea after another popped into my head; a vampire chasing him, no possibility of escape, a scream. I was still writing furiously when the period ended.

Mr. Bratspies, my fifth-grade teacher... was definitely the coolest grown-up at Whittier School.... I remember feeling I'd discovered some hidden secret as we analyzed the lyrics to Simon and Garfunkel's "Sounds of Silence."

Mr. Bratspies stopped at my desk, seeming to sense my excitement. "So, what's going on here?" he asked. This was long before the days of writing workshop; the expectation was that you started and finished a story in the same sitting.

I began telling my idea that this boy was just the first victim of a large cadre of vampires and the story was going to be narrated by his father who wanted to get revenge and there would be a war of the humans against the vampires but in the end the father would fail because too many stories have happy endings and that's predictable and boring.

Mr. Bratspies smiled at my breathless explanation. "Sounds like there's a lot you want to put in there," he said, genuinely interested. "I see you're writing the part about the boy now. How is that going?"

I answered that I was trying to make it scary and exciting, but didn't want to give away that it was a vampire chasing him right at the start. "Interesting," he responded. "Why do you want to wait to tell about that?"

The question took me back. No one had ever asked me before about my intentions as a writer. Feeling pretty important (my favorite teacher was actually interested in what I was thinking!), I answered that waiting would make it more suspenseful. It was a word I knew from television.

"Hmmm," he replied. "Sounds like you know something about how scary stories go. It sounds like you're thinking about the way you want your reader to feel. Is that right?"

Before Mr. Bratspies said it, I never realized I'd been thinking about how I wanted my reader to feel. But yes, that was right.

I responded by saying there would be lots of other feelings later in the story. When the father finds his son is dead, the story would feel sad, then the reader should feel mad at the vampires. After a while, of course, there would be excitement about the war. Mr. Bratspies suggested that I hold on to my piece and work on it longer. He asked if I'd like to look at some books together, to figure out ways authors can make readers feel different things across a long story.

> "Every child has a story to tell. The question is, will he tell it to you?"
> **—HAROLD ROSEN**

Vampire Valhalla ended up being 35 single-spaced pages, typed up by my mother and written over the course of three weeks. I later learned Mr. Bratspies read it annually to Whittier School's incoming fifth-grade students for the next decade.

The significant thing here is not my early brush with literary fame. What stuck was how this teacher saw beyond a 10-year-old's horror movie plotline, identified a beginning understanding of how stories work, and responded with a next step to teach the young writer something about writing and reading. Just as important, he made me feel my thoughts were worth pursuing.

*

Though Mr. Bratspies was never trained in reading or writing workshop, he instinctively knew that the way to reach the 10-year-old, would-be horror story author in front of him was to prioritize and value what he was trying to accomplish. This is rare in suburban, largely White communities and international schools, and even less common in urban schools serving mostly students of color.

As Christopher Emdin (2016) describes it, "...urban youth are expected to leave their day-to-day experiences and emotions at the door and assimilate into the culture of schools." In other words, the student is expected to adapt to the institution, not the other way around. When the institution fails to acknowledge the reality of the individual child—or worse, suggests the child's reality is somehow inferior or less valid—the result can be traumatic. In the words of Frederick Douglass, "Once you learn to read, you will be forever free"—but if the person teaching you to read and write is not interested in understanding you or your ideas, reading and writing can feel like a shackle thrust upon you. To achieve equity in a reading and writing workshop, it is critical that "every individual is perceived as having a distinct perspective and is given the opportunity to express that in the classroom." (Emdin again!)

Conferring is by definition one-on-one teaching. When approached through an equity lens rather than as a means to cover predetermined content, there is no better way to validate each student's distinct perspective. Further, sharing and celebrating individual conferring work can provide natural opportunities to express and validate the unique reading and writing personalities that live in every classroom.

The key to conferring successfully is listening to children, but in a different way than we may be used to. Naturally it is important to assess through the lens of standards and year-end expectations—but it's also critical to understand who each individual student is as a reader and writer. What unique perspective does this fifth grader bring to the book she is reading today, or to books in general? What craft moves does this third grader notice his favorite author using, and is he beginning to try them in his own writing? "There are many ways for us to convey information to kids," JoAnn Portalupi advises. "A conference is one place they can convey information to us."

The not-so-subliminal message we send with this sort of listening is yes, your thoughts matter. As one conference connects to the next, a relationship of trust is established that develops and grows as new ideas are discovered and explored. Some of the most meaningful moments in life are when we feel understood by another person. Moreover, feeling listened to—*really* listened to—can help us understand ourselves in ways we didn't understand before.

Some of the most meaningful moments in life are when we feel understood by another person. Moreover, feeling listened to—really listened to—can help us understand ourselves in ways we didn't understand before.

In addition to providing meaningful entry points for teaching, conferences also help children become aware of their own identities as readers and writers. Once they regard themselves as members of the literacy club, students become more engaged in their own learning. Consequently, they want to explore, expand, and develop the ideas that come up in conferences. After all, they helped come up with them.

There are, of course, many ways to listen. I've found that four, in particular, open doors for students *and* teachers.

Four Principles of Listening in Reading and Writing Conferences

1. Concentrate on learning before you worry about teaching.
2. Be curious. Ask questions.
3. Listen for the strength, not the deficit.
4. Listen for the general in the specific.

1 Concentrate on learning before you worry about teaching.

One of the greatest sources of anxiety for teachers when they sit down to confer is deciding the perfect thing to teach. There are so many choices—curriculum objectives, standards for the grade, goals for specific students indicated by formal and informal assessments. What is the most appropriate thing to address *today*? It's easy to second-guess our decisions and feel enormous pressure to get it right.

While it's always a good idea for a teacher to think ahead of what she knows about a student—strengths, struggles, possible directions—in the first couple of minutes of a conference, it is wise to prioritize learning over teaching. In this particular moment, what is this student thinking about, struggling with, excited about? Is there anything I recognize as a pattern? Of course, we want to address goals for individual children, but it's important to not let these good intentions get in the way of listening to and learning from the student.

Many teachers find it liberating to spend time at the beginning of a conference consciously avoiding thinking about any teaching point at all. Instead, they allow themselves the luxury of listening carefully and taking notes on what the student is saying and doing in the moment.

Jason Coleman, a fifth-grade teacher at the International School of Ghana, tells of the pressure he felt in his early conferences. "I was driving myself crazy worrying about finding the right thing to teach, to the point where I wasn't even listening to the kid! So I decided to start the next year going one round of conferences without teaching them *anything*. I just listened to each student and took notes," he explains. "It was amazing how much more relaxed I felt on the second round! Because of those first conferences, I had lots of ideas about possible directions, and was able to really focus on what the student was saying. It was much easier to come up with meaningful teaching points."

② Be curious. Ask questions.

Most of us became teachers, at least in part, because we are interested in the way children think. Sadly, as the realities of accountability, school and district mandates, and standardized testing take over, it's easy to lose sight of this initial passion. With so little time and so much to cover, we understandably feel too much pressure from above to allow ourselves the luxury of curiosity.

Yet, if our objective is to find the most effective entry point for individual students, being curious about what they are thinking is no luxury—it is a necessity. "Childhood has its own way of seeing, thinking, and feeling," cautioned Jean-Jacques Rousseau in his seminal 1762 study *Emile, or On Education*, "and nothing is more foolish than to try to substitute ours for theirs." In other words, children are not just miniature adults—and it's a mistake to assume we can help them *to* understand without first figuring out *how* they understand. "The logic by which we teach," Glenda Bissix (1980) reminds us, "is not always the logic by which children learn."

If our objective is to find the most effective entry point for individual students, being curious about what they are thinking is no luxury—it is a necessity.

Conferences give us the opportunity to reclaim that fascination with children's minds we felt when entering the field. Taking the time to be curious is a win-win. The student feels honored that a significant adult is paying attention, and the adult gets to enjoy each child's unique perspective. (No small thing—shouldn't this work be fun?) Formal assessments (e.g., Fountas & Pinnell Benchmark Assessment Systems, DIBELS) yield meaningful information about young readers and writers, but they are only part of the picture; how that data does or doesn't dovetail with what we observe up close and personal fills in the blanks.

One way to channel your curiosity productively is to ask students to elaborate on their initial thinking, rather than jumping in or moving on after the first words they say. Usually when children are asked to share ideas in school, they haltingly express a thought, and the teacher quickly moves on to the next volunteer. But as Ellin Keene (2012) points out, the first thing out of anyone's mouth is rarely their best thinking. Chances are if a phrase, idea, or word choice strikes the teacher as interesting, it is worth asking the child to elaborate. A general rule of thumb is to listen for the most interesting parts of what a student says, and ask her to "say more about that" *at least three times* before leaping in with teacher content. It may sound formulaic, but it's surprising how much a child's thinking deepens exponentially with this simple move. (Don't take my word—try it yourself!)

When you take the time to be curious and ask questions, it is a signal that you care what the child is thinking. As a result, you are able to establish a personal connection that pays off in the conference and beyond. Children are more likely to feel comfortable taking chances and pushing themselves further when they feel an adult is there to listen and understand, rather than judge and assess.

③ Listen for the strength, not the deficit.

When a teacher sits one-on-one with a child, the usual tendency is to listen for what that student *can't* do. With so little time to address individual needs, doesn't it make sense to help kids with their struggles on those rare occasions when no one else is around? Yet it's important to keep in mind that if the usual subject of a conference is what the student does *least* well, that child is not going to look forward to the conversation.

The sweet spot in teaching is figuring out what a learner is just *beginning* to understand, but needs scaffolding to become independent—and then follow that lead. Lev Vygotsky calls this the zone of proximal development, or ZPD—"the level of potential development as determined through problem-solving under adult guidance (1978)." Another way of thinking about this, as Carl Anderson describes in *A Teacher's Guide to Writing Conferences* (2019), is "listening for the partial understanding." What is this young reader or writer starting to notice that he or she can't quite name? Which part of what that student said suggests a next step for teaching?

Put simply, it is usually more effective to confer to the strength than the deficit. This takes practice to be sure. It's a shift away from our usual mindset of prioritizing what the student does *not* know. But when we get in the habit of listening for a partial understanding and using that as the jumping-off point for instruction, the results can be powerful and lasting. Perhaps a second grader writing a personal narrative wants to "make this part more exciting," but isn't yet aware he can accomplish this by slowing down the action; maybe a sixth grader knows the latest event in her book speaks to a larger theme, but doesn't yet understand she could go deeper into the idea by connecting to what happened earlier in the text.

Recognizing what a student is starting to think about, putting a name on it, and then suggesting a way to go further, makes the learning (and teaching) feel like a collaborative effort. And from the child's point of view, when the teaching point comes from something she is noticing, it creates a feeling of ownership. She begins to look forward to the next conference.

> *When we get in the habit of listening for a partial understanding and using that as the jumping-off point for instruction, the results can be powerful and lasting.*

4 Listen for the general in the specific.

Children are concrete thinkers. "The child often sees only what he already knows," suggests Piaget (1954). When it comes to literacy, today's writing lesson is only about today's piece of writing; the current reading lesson is only about the book we are reading at this moment.

It's easy for teachers to look through a similar lens. After all, a few specific suggestions would really improve this persuasive essay; and highlighting the character traits of the protagonist would surely help the class to understand today's read-aloud. The problem is, when students move on to the next piece of writing or to their next book, they often don't see how the strategy from yesterday's lesson connects to today's work.

It's not that there is no value in pointing out specific examples in the writing or the book we are working with today—indeed, if our teaching isn't grounded in the specific, the student is unlikely to know what we are talking about. But the key move if we want our teaching to stick is to *start with the specific and then move to the general*. In other words, to help students understand how what we taught them today can apply to the *next* book or piece of writing. To make the teaching point *transferable*.

Lucy Calkins reminds us to "Teach the writer, not the writing." It is more important for a fifth grader to learn something from today's personal narrative that she can bring to her future writing than it is to perfect the current story. Similarly, the priority should be to *teach the reader, not the book*. It's unlikely that a fourth grader will fall behind in his ability to comprehend if he misses some of the nuances in Matt de la Peña's *Last Stop on Market Street*; what matters is that he takes something from this reading experience to apply to the next book, and the book after that.

Radical listening means being present, being curious, and being diagnostic— but perhaps most importantly, it is an invitation for the student to be an active participant in his or her own learning.

When we discuss why it's important to notice Nate the Great's traits, a second grader is likely to think that's a neat thing to do when you read *Nate the Great*. At the age of seven, he probably won't realize that paying attention to the way characters act is helpful in understanding any story. When we teach a sixth grader to follow a long sentence with a short one to emphasize an important point in her personal essay, she is likely to walk away thinking that's a nifty trick to use in *this* personal essay. She may not understand it's a writing strategy you can use in other genres as well.

Listening to specifics with an eye toward the general is for many teachers the most challenging part of conferring well. To do this effectively, we must (again) listen for the partial understanding, usually something specific to today's book or piece of writing—and then build on it. When articulating this teaching point, it's important to use general, *transferable* language that can apply to future reading or writing. For example, rather than just pointing out the way E.B. White's description of the barn creates a lonely feeling in *Charlotte's Web*, we may use that as an opportunity to teach how setting can convey a mood in other books as well.

For students to become independent readers and writers, they need a repertoire of strategies that can be used across many types of books and different kinds of writing. Listening for specifics in a conference, with an eye toward teaching something general and transferable, is one powerful, personal way to help children make such connections.

*

These four principles of listening, though distinct, all involve being responsive *and* proactive at the same time. None of them are passive. We are allowing students to convey information to us, validating it, and at the same time nudging them to go further in their thinking.

At a recent professional institute, Carl Anderson, Cornelius Minor, and I gave a presentation called "Rules for Radical Listening." Though I hesitate to think of it in terms of rules, the very idea of listening to children this way is radical in many schools, even "progressive" ones—and certainly in the larger world. (As one example, it's striking how many adults actually answer *for* their children when someone asks them a question!) The radical aspect of conferring comes from listening to children in such a way that what they say and do becomes just as important as what we say and do.

To confer well with young readers and writers, it's essential to begin from a position of mutual respect and trust. When we convey to a child that his or her words are interesting and important, that child begins to open up and take chances. This sort of radical listening means being present, being curious, and being diagnostic—but perhaps most importantly, it is an invitation for the student to be an active participant in his or her own learning.

Teacher Kimberley Fung confers with a student at the Ming Yang My WordPlay Reading and Writing Workshop in Shenzhen, China.

Conferring Basics

"Reading is the inhale; writing is the exhale."
—Mary K. Tedrow

First things first. There are books about individual writing conferences, and books about individual reading conferences. Though they are often discussed separately, in the day-to-day life of a classroom, any teacher doing one is also doing the other. More importantly, any child who is learning to read is also learning to write.

Reading and writing are mirror images, and being skilled at one deepens our understanding of the other. "Writing comes from reading," says novelist Annie Proulx, "and reading is the finest teacher of how to write." Similarly, when young readers look at text through the lens of *how the author wrote it*, they are better positioned to understand. As Colleen Cruz (2020) succinctly puts it, "For every comprehension move a reader makes, there is an author on the other side of the desk." The answer to a writing question can often be solved by looking at how a favorite author did it. And the answer to a reading comprehension question might be found by thinking about the author's choices; if she put that detail in this place, it probably means it's important.

Conferring provides powerful opportunities to make these connections explicit. And if you're doing reading and writing conferences with the same group of students, the good news is that for all their differences, many of the basic moves are the same.

Before delving deeply into the unique characteristics of writing and reading conferences, in this chapter we'll look at what makes them the same and different.

What's the Difference Between a Writing Conference and a Reading Conference?

Probably the most obvious difference between a writing and reading conference has to do with evidence. Conferring with a student in writing usually involves something concrete, or visible. Most of the time, there is actual work to look at, even if the student is a reluctant talker. In contrast, reading comprehension is invisible; once children move past sounding out words, understanding and coming up with ideas about text happens inside their heads. In a reading conference, we must learn strategies for finding an instructional direction without the help of concrete evidence.

Then there is the specific content. Writing conferences are about teaching qualities of writing. For example, we might talk about how and when to add detail, teach characteristics of a genre, how to structure a piece, or use conventions.

We may also teach stages of the writing process; the work of a writer depends, at least in part, on whether she or he is planning, drafting, revising, or proofreading.

On the other hand, a reading conference often deals with metacognitive strategies, what we do in our head to make meaning (e.g., when to prioritize, make connections, infer, or monitor for meaning). It may also focus on text-based content, such as story elements or informational text features.

Though many places in the Venn diagram of literacy overlap, there's no getting around the fact that there are different things to learn about reading and writing.

What's the Same?

In the big picture, both types of conferences help students learn to make independent choices. In writing, where does it make sense to include examples in a persuasive essay, or add sensory description to a story? In reading, how do we know which details reveal a character's motivation, or what facts in a feature article are important to remember? Individual conferences are ideal opportunities to teach students to be reading and writing decision-makers.

Another important similarity between the two types of conferences has to do with their ultimate purpose. In reading, it's less important for a student to understand every nuance of a book than to take something from it that she can bring to the next book, and the book after that. In a writing conference, we hope to leave a student with a strategy that can apply to future writing as well as the current piece. In both, the objective is to teach a lesson that is transferable, not just about today's work but something that will add to a child's repertoire moving forward. Teach the reader, not the book; teach the writer, not the writing.

We look for similar points of entry in a reading and a writing conference. For the lesson to stick, it's important to start where a student is *beginning* to understand but can't quite do independently—that good ol' zone of proximal development. One way of thinking about this is that it's easier to see the end of the road if you've already begun the trip.

Whether it's reading or writing, a conference follows a similar three-part structure. As Lucy Calkins (1994) succinctly puts it:

- Research the child.
- Out of that research, make an instructional decision.
- Teach something to help the student become a better reader or writer.

"Research/decide/teach" has become a mantra for educators learning the art of conferring, but it's useful to think a bit more deeply about these steps. In *A Teacher's Guide to Writing Conferences* (2018), Carl Anderson describes these three parts of a conference a bit differently:

- Discover what the student is working on as a writer, or thinking about as a reader. Sometimes this will be obvious; more often, we have to probe.
- Assess where the student is in her or his understanding. If she is beginning to write complex sentences, which punctuation is she using, and how? If he is starting to make inferences in a realistic fiction novel, are they about character traits, or larger themes?
- Decide on a next step related to that partial understanding to teach something useful about reading or writing.

"Research/decide/teach" can also be thought of as "discover/assess/teach."

The similarities and differences between reading and writing conferences are summed up in the following chart.

What's the Same (and Different) About Writing Conferences and Reading Conferences?

A Writing Conference...	A Reading Conference...
• *Usually* deals with something visual, such as a piece of writing.	• Deals with the invisible (comprehension happens inside our heads).
• Is the most effective place to teach strategies for thinking through each stage of the writing process, as well as the qualities of writing.	• Is the most effective place to teach comprehension strategies in reading.
• From the teacher's point of view, has a three-part structure: research (discover)/decide (assess)/teach something useful about writing.	• From the teacher's point of view, has a three-part structure: research (discover)/decide (assess)/teach something useful about reading.
• Typically focuses on a partial understanding—we identify what a writer is trying to do or could benefit from learning, and teach from there.	• Typically focuses on a partial understanding—we identify what a reader is on the edge of being able to do on her own, and teach from there.
• Is the best place to teach students to become writing decision-makers.	• Is the best place to teach students to become comprehension decision-makers.
• Should focus on teaching the writer, not the writing (Calkins, 1994).	• Should focus on teaching the reader, not the book.

Conferring Competencies

Recently, while preparing to present at a conference for the International School of Kuala Lumpur, Director of Learning Praxia Apostle asked me to create a rubric breaking down the skill sets a teacher needs to confer effectively. At first I resisted. The idea of characterizing a teacher's progress on a trajectory from low to high felt contrary to the spirit of a conference. Grudgingly, I began making some notes.

Once past my initial resistance, I had to admit there are things to know and be able to do to confer well—and there's often a predictable progression a teacher goes through as she learns and improves. I began to change my mind about the rubric. As long as we weren't thinking in terms of good or bad, looking at conferring competencies as a continuum felt like it could be a helpful way to improve and move from one step to the next (see Art of Conferring Rubric on page 29).

Just as a doctor listens to a patient and knows the questions to ask to determine an appropriate treatment, a teacher must know how to listen to a student to figure out the best entry point for teaching something useful about reading or writing.

Whether it's a reading conference or a writing conference, there are three skill sets we must draw on. Though some of the specifics vary depending on the type of conference we are talking about, the broad categories are the same. I'll call these "conferring competencies."

Competency 1: *Content Knowledge* Carl Anderson points out the irony of referring to math, science, and social studies as "the content areas"—as if they were the only ones. The truth is there's concrete stuff to know about reading comprehension strategies and the qualities of good writing as well. To confer effectively, we need to be familiar with content—and convey it to a student in such a way that the lesson goes beyond today's book or piece of writing. In the next two chapters, I'll go over some of these strategies.

Competency 2: *Diagnostic Listening* It isn't enough to just hear a student's words, nod, and press on with a predetermined lesson. Conferring is responsive teaching, understanding and responding to a child at a particular moment in time. Just as a doctor listens to a patient and knows the questions to ask to determine an appropriate treatment, a teacher must know how to listen to a student to figure out the best entry point for teaching something useful about reading or writing.

Competency 3: *Structure, Sequence, and Pacing* This refers to how and when we move from one part of the conference to the next. One way to look at structure is through the lens of discover/assess/teach (or research/decide/teach, if you prefer), as discussed earlier. Another way of thinking about it is moving back and forth from specific to general. The conference begins by discussing today's *specific* book or writing, then moves on to a *general*, transferable teaching point which can apply to future reading or writing. Next, with the student, we determine work to do in the current *specific* text or writing piece to practice the new skill or strategy. Finally, we restate this *general* teaching point and explain how it will help with reading or writing moving forward.

Specific	Talk about what the student is thinking about today's book or working on in today's piece of writing.
General	Make a teaching point in general, transferable language that can apply to other texts or writing pieces.
Specific	Negotiate an assignment to practice the teaching point as the student begins to read or write.
General	Remind the student of the teaching point, and how doing this work will help her/him in future reading or writing.

In a successful conference, these three competencies play off one another. We listen with a diagnostic lens, then match a child's thinking to her content knowledge, e.g., a comprehension strategy or quality of writing. (Did that comment about Amber Brown's actions in this chapter sound like inference, or was he connecting details across the text? Does this young writer's attempt to add examples to her essay suggest a lesson on structure or elaboration?) After choosing an instructional direction, we decide when to continue to the next step in the conference (e.g., from the specific to the general, or from assessment to teaching).

As intertwined as they are, these competencies are separate skills—and most teachers do not feel equally confident in all three. As with any new learning, there are predictable phases within each competency that most of us go through on the road to conferring expertise.

In the area of *content knowledge*, it's typical to start by just thinking about the current book or writing piece. With more practice, teachers begin to address more general, grade-specific lessons. Finally, we feel more comfortable (and competent) at targeting instruction to the individual child, whether the teaching point dovetails with a whole-class lesson.

As for *diagnostic listening*, in the beginning stages most teachers talk too much (an occupational hazard!), and don't allow the child enough airtime. After a while, the student gets to say more, but conferences still address predetermined instructional goals that may or may not apply to individual strengths and needs. Eventually, we become more skilled at eliciting student thinking, and better able to match what children say or do to a teaching point tailored to the reader and writer in front of them.

When it comes to *structure*, *sequence*, and *pacing*, at first a conference is often approached as a free-flowing chat, with no sequence or steps involved. Next comes a general awareness of the research/decide/teach (discover/assess/teach) arc that distinguishes it from other sorts of conversations. At a certain point, we develop a sense of when and how to move from one part of the conference to the next, in a way that feels natural and purposeful.

For teachers looking to make conferring an integral part of their reading and writing instruction, it can be helpful to set short- (or long-) term goals in each specific competency—and consider how they work together in an actual conference. Though growth in any skill or subject rarely follows an identical trajectory from one person to the next, a typical progression may be found in the following chart.

ART OF CONFERRING RUBRIC				
Conferring Competencies	**Beginning**	**Developing**	**Applying**	**Strategic** Thinking Across Reading and Writing
Content Knowledge (qualities of writing; comprehension strategies)	Addresses issues in reading conferences that are text-specific (e.g., correcting literal misunderstandings in a book), and piece-specific in writing conferences (e.g., fixing grammatical errors in today's writing), rather than making teaching points generalizable to future reading and writing.	Is able to name grade-appropriate qualities of writing, and/or comprehension strategies in reading—and sometimes apply them to the strengths and needs of a particular student.	Is able to identify and prioritize appropriate teaching points in reading and writing, and then match them to strengths and needs of an individual child.	Is able to identify and prioritize appropriate teaching points for an individual child that help her/him see connections between reading and writing, i.e., to "read like a writer and write like a reader."
Diagnostic Listening	Confers with an imbalanced ratio of teacher-to-student talk; lacks strategies to draw out and elicit student thinking.	Approaches a conference as a place to teach predetermined curriculum goals for the grade or unit, rather than taking cues from the individual child.	Is able to make appropriate instructional decisions based on what a student says and does in a conference, as well as considering long-term individual goals for that child.	Can listen to and elicit thinking from a student that suggests possible reading and writing connections, and then follow up with appropriate teaching points.
Structure, Sequence, and Pacing	Confers with no structure in mind, and/or as a review/remedial session related to a whole-class lesson.	Has a general sense of the research-decide-teach arc of a conferring conversation.	Confers with an appropriate structure and sequence in mind, in this order: • listening • eliciting further student thinking • teaching an individually targeted strategy or skill • giving the student appropriate, engaging work to practice and apply.	Confers with an appropriate structure and sequence in mind (see descriptors in "Applying"), with conscious attempts to connect teaching points across reading and writing conferences.

Over time, as each competency progresses, it becomes possible to not just teach reading and writing strategies separately, but to consistently link the two. At this point, conferences have the potential to help students "read like writers, and write like readers" independently, and begin to see connections on their own. As children get the message that their individual ideas and noticings are driving the instruction, the level of engagement in a classroom increases dramatically.

Just as importantly, students start to think of reading and writing as ways to express who they are, where they come from, and what they have to say. Literacy becomes personal, not something unrelated to their lives and thrust upon them. By first honoring the individual experiences and backgrounds in our classrooms, we can point children to ideas and worlds they might not otherwise discover. Reading and writing conferences can help children figure out who they are and want to be in the world.

Logistical FAQs

As with almost anything in teaching, it's the nitty-gritty classroom management stuff that will make or break you—and individual reading and writing conferences are no exception. What follows are some thoughts about how to deal with these concerns and create a predictable and productive routine, for both teacher and student.

How many conferences should I aim for in a day?

A typical conference is about five to eight minutes long and usually takes place when students are engaged in independent work. In a reading or writing workshop with 20 to 25 minutes of independent work time, this usually means three to four conferences.

And now, the caveats. As we get used to the structure of a conference and begin to practice new habits of listening, our early attempts will almost always be longer than we'd like. Even for an experienced teacher, first conferences of the year with a new group of students are usually closer to eight to 10 minutes in length. Have faith! After a conference or two with a student, it is much easier to stay in the five- to eight-minute range—especially if we start to think ahead about possible directions.

If every child is working on something different, how do I keep track of their assignments?

Apart from developing a system for note-taking (more on that in the next chapter), it can be useful to set up a wall calendar or chart in the room where students record their assignments and due dates. This has the double benefit of being a quick place to look for reminders of who has what due when, and also allows students to see what others are working on.

(top) Wall calendar to keep track of conferring work from Katie Vis's fifth-grade classroom at International School of Latvia

(right) Bulletin board for keeping track of reading conference work-in-progress from the Hong Kong International School

Where should I confer?

To a certain extent, this is a matter of personal preference. My colleague Sharon Taberski likes to set up a special table where students come when it is their turn. She argues that it makes them feel special, and the conversations more private. I prefer to confer with children wherever they are sitting in the room. If others overhear the conference, it provides more bang for the buck. Often the kid sitting one seat over can benefit from the teaching point of her neighbor; but even if not, at the very least she will begin to internalize how a conference conversation goes (the type of questions, what it means to think about your thinking, and so on). In this way, she will be more prepared when her turn comes.

What are some tips for fitting in as many conferences as possible in a single instructional period?

It can be helpful to plan which students you are going to confer with on a given day, taking into consideration:

- where children are sitting. (To aid in classroom management, it's best to move around the room and not stay in one place the entire period.)
- who they have or haven't seen recently. (We don't want to have two conferences with Anwar in a week when we haven't seen Laila once.)
- how long to spend with each reader or writer. (Making time goals in advance can help us be more efficient. For example, Lashawn is sailing along and I have a pretty good idea where the conference might go, so I plan for five minutes. But Keisha has been struggling lately and I'll need more time with her, so that conference will be eight minutes.)
- notes from previous conferences. (Taking a few minutes before today's conference to look over what you talked about last time can help formulate ideas for possible next steps.)

CHAPTER THREE

Individual Reading Conferences

"Read to make yourself smarter! Less judgmental. More apt to understand your friends' insane behavior, or better yet, your own."

—**John Waters**

"I'm just thinking about if I was there right now," says fourth grader Zaima, her eyes sparkling as she indicates the paperback in front of her of Aisha Saeed's *Amal Unbound*. "It's about this girl called Amal. She's actually from Pakistan like me, which is why I picked up this book. Because of the story of that kind of girl."

Her teacher at the Hong Kong Peak School, Sarah Cheng, nods and asks Zaima to say more. "Well, she lives somewhere in a part of Pakistan, which I do, too. She doesn't live in Islamabad, but she lives in Punjab, which is another province next to Islamabad. She's not exactly like me, her village is really very small, but it's near Islamabad"—she motions excitedly with her hands to show the distance—"and they both have the same sort of markets, like with small stalls."

> "You think your pain and your heartbreak are unprecedented in the history of the world, but then you read. It was books that taught me that the things that tormented me most were the very things that connected me with all the people who were alive, or who had ever been alive."
> —JAMES BALDWIN

Vernette, a sixth-grade student at Satellite Middle School in Bedford-Stuyvesant, Brooklyn, is sharing her ideas about Sandra Cisneros's short story "Eleven" with teacher Sonya Simpson. "It was about how even though your birthday comes around and you've aged, there are going to come moments where you're not going to *act* your age. You're going to burst out and do childish things." Her mouth curls into a smile as she continues. "I'm 12, but I act more like I'm five. I like watching television shows for one-year-olds. I say 'meow.' I like hugs. I run around like a little baby looking for attention. People say act your age, but I say you can't act your age! You want to be happy and you want to be childish."

Second grader Shaquan's book basket is filled with picture books about artists: *Radiant Child* is a colorful biography of Jean-Michel Basquiat; *Frida Kahlo and Her "Animalitos"* describes how the Mexican painter was inspired by her pets. Monique, Shaquan's teacher at a Harlem, New York charter school, asks about his choices. Shaquan shyly pulls out a pile of crayon drawings from his desk. "I like these books because I want to be an artist," he answers in a quiet voice.

Ava, an eighth-grade student at Mt. Zaagkam school in Papua, Indonesia, frowns as she discusses the YA novel *Never Fall Down* with Amy Richie, her ELA teacher. "What the author has done, the way the ending works, is he's resolved the external conflict of Arn surviving the cruelty of the Khmer Rouge, but then introduced an internal conflict of him trying to figure out how to deal with regular life after that, going to normal high school." She shakes her head. "This really makes me think about how sometimes people never get over stuff."

What Makes Us Want to Read?

Before getting into the specifics of reading conferences, it makes sense to think about their larger purpose. That means stepping back and considering what makes a person want to read in the first place.

It might be to not feel alone in the world, like Zaima seeking out stories of other Pakistani girls. Maybe it's to clarify your thinking on issues that matter, as when Vernette compared her own ideas about aging to those of Sandra Cisneros. Sometimes it's to explore who we want to become, like Shaquan did in choosing books about artists. A text can also help us understand and feel empathy for lives and experiences we don't know firsthand, as Ava experienced reading *Never Fall Down*.

In each conference, those young readers were invited to recognize and extend something within themselves. When we feel this sort of ownership, reading feels very different than when we are told what to think about. We read to learn about things we care about, and to think through things that confuse us. We read to cry and laugh and feel angry. We read because it helps us figure out who we are. As Rudine Sims Bishop (1990) puts it, "Books are sometimes windows, offering views of worlds that may be real or imagined, familiar or strange. These windows are also sliding glass doors, and readers have only to walk through in imagination to become part of whatever world has been created or recreated by the author. When lighting conditions are just right, however, a window can also be a mirror... and in that reflection we can see our own lives and experiences as part of the larger human experience."

Each of these purposes involves a back and forth between a text and the beliefs and experiences of the person reading it. In the words of Louise Rosenblatt (1978), a book is "just ink on a page until the reader comes along and gives it life." What a text means to an individual reader is no more or less important as understanding its literal meaning.

This is not just a poetic way of looking at comprehension. Gholdy Muhammad, in *Cultivating Genius* (2020), recounts how in the 19th century, African Americans formed literary societies of their own in response to anti-literacy laws and policies. They defined one of their primary goals, or learning pursuits, as identity development through literacy. When we consciously balance what-the-words-on-the-page-say with what-you-the-reader-thinks, not prioritizing one over the other, students feel more engaged and think more deeply. They also develop a sense of their own individual reading personality. Am I the sort of reader who compares my decisions to those of the main character? Do I tend to question the facts an author includes in an editorial, before deciding on my own point of view?

When each reader's ideas and identities are given equal airtime in a classroom, comprehension instruction can be a democracy of thought.

Reading conferences can be at once about extending the thinking of the child in front of us, and creating a community of readers who learn from each other. Though they are, by definition, one-to-one teaching, it's a mistake to think of conferences as private and confidential. When students have regular opportunities to hear the perspectives of other readers in the class, they gain new ways of experiencing text and thinking about the world. Through accessing the spark in each student and taking time to celebrate the class's diversity of ideas, children widen their own comprehension repertoire and learn to appreciate other points of view. When each reader's ideas and identities are given equal airtime in a classroom, comprehension instruction can be a democracy of thought.

The objective of a reading conference is to teach into these real-life purposes. Together with making sense of the words on the page, children learn to recognize, deepen, and extend their own lines of thinking, backing up their ideas with text evidence. Along the way, they develop their identities as thinkers—and understand the importance of being open to other points of view.

Breaking It Down: What Is an Individual Reading Conference?

A great jazz sax solo can sound as if it came out of thin air, created spontaneously in the moment. On one level, this is true; there is no sheet music indicating exactly which notes to play. At the same time, the musician is paying attention to the song's chords, anticipating where the key changes from major to minor, knowing what will fit within each section. There is no exact plan, but to make it work the sax player improvises within a structure, calling on his content knowledge of music theory.

At first listen, a reading conference can sound like a spontaneous conversation about a book, with no road map or plan. On one level, that is true. After all, a conference is, by definition, responsive teaching; there's no script with exact words to say. But like the jazz soloist, to confer powerfully we must improvise within a conversational structure, calling on our content knowledge of reading comprehension.

The idea of using those two skill sets simultaneously while actively listening to a child in a conference may seem intimidating at first. Happily, most teachers not only rise to the challenge but also find with practice that conferring this way becomes the most meaningful form of comprehension instruction in their repertoire.

Before thinking about how it all comes together, let's look at the content of comprehension and the structure of a reading conference separately.

The Content of Comprehension: What We Teach When We Teach Reading

So what exactly is the content of comprehension? In subjects such as math, science, and social studies, it's clear what content means; there are facts, formulas, strategies, and ideas to learn. When it comes to reading, it's less obvious. For one thing, there are critical issues around culture and language—where a child comes from, what her first language is—that play into the meaning-making process. (I'll get into some of those issues later when discussing diagnostic tips.) In *Reading Projects Reimagined* (2015), I suggest that to come up with a teaching point in a reading conference, two categories need to be prioritized: metacognitive strategies and text-based content.

First, there are the things we do in our head to make meaning. These *metacognitive strategies* include determining importance, inferring, and monitoring for meaning—what an experienced reader often does without even realizing it, but a child just learning to read is still learning. Ellin Keene (2007) refers to these as "deep structure systems," to distinguish them from word work.

Then there is *text-based content*, what's on the page and *not* in the reader's head. Examples of this include story elements, informational text features, and literary devices such as metaphor and simile.

When we guide young readers to think in terms of those categories, they begin to understand more deeply and come up with their own ideas about text (Duke, Pearson, Strachan, & Billman, 2011). For example, while reading a novel, we might infer the problem is going to get worse before it gets better, based on our knowledge of story elements. When thinking about a news article, we are likely to prioritize the facts in the first two paragraphs, based on our knowledge of how news articles are written.

The teaching point in a reading conference focuses on one or more of the things in these two categories. As we listen to students talk about their books, it's important to consider what makes the best entry point. Specifically, are there metacognitive strategies the reader is ready to go further with? Based on the child's current understanding, are there opportunities for teaching something more text-based? Though a teacher may (and should!) come to the conference with instructional goals in mind, it's important to be open to what the student is thinking about and noticing today.

To make wise decisions about anything, you have to know your choices. This is just as true in a reading conference as anywhere else. To decide on a direction for a reader, it's necessary to know the content of comprehension. What follows is a cheat sheet, summarizing some (not all) of the possibilities.

CONTENT OF COMPREHENSION: A CHEAT SHEET FOR CONFERRING

METACOGNITIVE STRATEGIES *What readers do in their heads*	TEXT-BASED CONTENT *What's on the page, not in readers' heads*
Prioritize Deciding what's more and less important.	**Story Elements** Plot, character, setting, movement through time, problem/solution/reflection.
Infer Reading between the lines, understanding what the author is implying without saying directly.	**Literary Devices** Such as metaphor, simile, personification, alliteration.
Question and Argue With the Text Not taking things at face value, e.g., noticing what information is left out of a news report, thinking a character action in a story is unrealistic.	**Punctuation** Such as exclamation marks, parentheses, em dashes, question marks.
Make Connections Accessing prior knowledge; connecting to personal experiences, other books, and/or things we know about in the world.	**Informational Text Features** Such as captions, subtitles, sidebars, italics.
Evoke Sensory and Emotional Images Visualizing what's happening in a text; imagining what it sounds, feels, or tastes like; feeling the feelings of a character, or the mood of the story.	**Informational Text Structures** How the text is written, such as problem/solution, cause/effect, question/answer.
Monitor for Meaning Knowing what to do when something in a text is confusing or complicated.	
Synthesize Connecting the dots, within or between texts e.g., understanding how something on the first page connects to a detail on the second page, or how an idea in one book connects to another.	

Adapted from *Mosaic of Thought* (Keene & Zimmerman, 2007)

Go to page 165 and scholastic.com/RadicalListeningResources for a reproducible/downloadable version of this sheet.

Structure of a Reading Conference: A Step-Wise Approach

It would be hard to find an artist who knew more about color than Picasso. The early years of his career were devoted to exploring hues and moods—the melancholy peasant subjects of the Blue Period, the playful clowns and carnival performers of the Rose Period.

And yet, for all his brilliance with color, in Picasso's paintings, content couldn't be separated from form. The most groundbreaking ideas in his work rest on a backbone of structure; the anti-war sentiments of *Guernica* expressed in jarring black-and-white contrast, the in-your-face presence of the women in *Les Demoiselles d'Avignon* heightened through purposely mismatched fragments. Even at its most abstract, Picasso's art was always grounded in a deep awareness of how each individual element related to the other elements. In other words, all that content knowledge of each separate thing—color, shape, perspective—only worked when communicated within a particular structure.

No matter how well you know your content—and no matter how varied the strengths and needs of individual students—what you teach in a conference is most powerfully conveyed by sticking to a conversational structure.

Just as math and science teachers need to know algorithms and basic scientific principles to teach those subjects, a reading teacher needs to know the content of comprehension. But no matter how well you know your content—and no matter how varied the strengths and needs of individual students—what you teach in a conference is most powerfully conveyed by sticking to a conversational structure. In broad strokes, it's the research/decide/teach sequence discussed in Chapter Two. But a closer look at how this plays out in a reading conference involves a series of specific steps.

Steps in a Reading Conference

RESEARCH AND DISCOVER

1. **Start with a thinking question,** e.g., "What are you thinking about [name of text]?" *Don't* begin by asking for a retell. This may be useful for the teacher, but is not engaging for the student.

2. **Listen for the most interesting thing the reader says or does,** and jot down her specific words or phrases. (If the student defaults to a retell/summary, listen for something that sounds like an idea or opinion.)

3. **If possible, name the reader's line of thinking** in general, transferable language that could apply to other books as well—and ask her to reflect on it, e.g., "It seems what you are doing as a reader is…am I right?"

4. **Ask the student to find a part in the book** that illustrates what she is noticing or thinking about.

5. **Ask the reader to say more about that thing.** Listen for the most interesting part of her response. Ask him/her to say more about *that*. (Ask some form of "Say more about that" at least three times before entering with your own content!)

ASSESS AND DECIDE

6. **Look and listen for a partial understanding.** Which comprehension strategy/strategies can you build on?

7. **Name the partial understanding in transferable language** that is about more than today's book, so it can be generalized as a strategy for future reading, e.g., "It seems like you are the type of reader who…."

TEACH

8. **State a teaching point that extends the partial understanding,** in language that can apply to the next book, and the book after that, e.g., "One important thing readers need to do is…"

9. **Negotiate concrete, specific work to do in today's text** to practice and extend the teaching point (e.g., sticky notes, reading notebook, graphic organizer). Have the students do a "try-it." Agree on how many, how long, due date, etc., for this assignment.

10. **Articulate the teaching point as a final comment, connecting it to future reading,** e.g., "Doing this work will help you practice…."

Go to page 166 and scholastic.com/RadicalListeningResources for a reproducible/downloadable version of these steps.

These steps and their order are not set in stone, by any means. Depending on the student, you may want to change the sequence here and there, double back and ask for a second example from the text, or vary in some other way. But this basic order works well to convey a teaching point so a student holds on to it beyond today's book.

A couple points of clarification:

- **"Say more about that" (Step 5):**
  The two-sided arrow between asking a child to "say more about that," listening for a partial understanding, and naming what she is doing as a reader indicates the importance of going back and forth between these steps. When we start naming what the child is doing as a reader, and then checking in (asking her to say more about that), we encourage the reader to be reflective and "think about her thinking" (Keene, 2007). It is a good idea to keep up this back-and-forth several times.

- **Assignment vs. Teaching Point (Steps 8–10):** One important thing to keep in mind in the latter part of a conference—during the "teach" section—is the distinction between an *assignment* and a *teaching point*. The *teaching point* is the larger lesson about reading (or writing!), which the student will learn and hopefully apply to future work. The *assignment* is the work we give the student today to practice, solidify, and extend that teaching point.

Conference With Amari

To imagine how this works in real life, it's helpful to look at a play-by-play of an actual reading conference and examine the teaching moves along the way. Though there are always variations in the teacher's style and in the student's reading personality (does anything in teaching ever go *exactly* as planned?), here's an example of how the steps unfolded with a soon-to-be third grader in New York City.

Amari is eight years old, nearing the end of second grade at a school in Harlem. This conference took place a couple of months after he had (proudly!) made the transition from picture books to chapter books.

DAN:	So Amari, you are reading *Hank the Cowdog*. Tell me what you're thinking about this book. **1**
AMARI:	So far I know that Hank is a dog that works a lot and does lots of stuff. That's pretty much all I know.
DAN:	*(Jots down "Hank works a lot.")* **2** Interesting. Tell me if I'm getting this right. It sounds like when you read stories, one of the things you do is learn who the characters are and find out as much important information about them as you can. Is that true? **3**
AMARI:	Mm-hmm.

1 I begin the conference with a *thinking question, not* a retell, which sets the expectation that the student is supposed to be doing the heavy lifting, actively coming up with ideas.

2 Here I *listen for the most interesting part* of what Amari says, and *jot down the phrase* "Hank works a lot" as it expresses a character trait observation—not a small thing for a second grader.

3 Early in the conference, I make the conversation as much about what Amari is doing as a reader as it is about the specifics of *Hank the Cowdog*. After *naming* it, I ask him to *reflect and confirm*—signaling that he should be thinking about his thinking.

DAN: You mentioned Hank is a dog that works a lot. How did you know that? **4**

AMARI: Because...I think it's on the first page...Here it is! It says *(reads aloud)*, "It's me again, Hank the Cowdog. I just got some terrible news. There's been a murder on the ranch! I know I shouldn't blame myself, but I mean a dog is only a dog. He can't be everywhere at once." So that tells me he does lots of work, because he's kind of complaining how he can't be everywhere at once.

DAN: Wow, you just did something interesting that I'm curious about. There wasn't anything in what you just read me that said "I do a lot of work," but you figured out that he does a lot of work from some of the other words. Can you tell me a little more about that? **5**

AMARI: Well, I kind of know that because since he can't be everywhere at once—like in my own life, my siblings tell me to do this and that when I'm only doing one thing.

4 5 Once you've found a line of thinking that seems promising, ask the student to "*Say more about that.*" (Do it more than once. As Ellin Keene (2012) asks, "How often is the first thing out of your mouth your best thinking?" It's the same for kids!) Here I've asked Amari to elaborate and to back up his thinking with evidence.

DAN: So you're connecting to your own life. Something you did there that was important, that readers always have to do, is read between the lines. It doesn't say he works a lot, but you get clues when he says things like he can't be everywhere at once, that tells you he works a lot. There's a fancy word for that—it's called when you *infer* something, when you figure out something the author did not say. **5** Are there any other

	places just in these first few pages where you figured out something the author didn't exactly say? **4**
AMARI:	Oh, I found one! It says, "You add that all up and you don't get Superman, just me. Good old easygoing Hank, who works hard and tries to do his job."

3 **4** **5** More naming, more "*Find a part*," more "*Say more about that*." Don't rush the research!

DAN:	There it is, about him working! So wait a minute—does that part connect to this part about how he can't be everywhere at once?
AMARI:	Mm-hmm.
DAN:	Connecting parts! Tell me about that. **5** **6** **7**
AMARI:	So, when I first read this page, a while ago, I didn't understand about I can't be everywhere at once, but then once I read that part, it told me. I thought that being everywhere at once sounds like working, so he probably works a lot.
DAN:	Wow. *(Dan jots down "At first I didn't understand...but then...)* **2** So, when you got to that second part you connected back to the first part, about being everywhere at once. *(Amari nods.)* You know, one of the things that readers have to do to read harder and harder books is decide which parts to connect. **8** Especially when you get into chapter books, authors expect the reader is going to know which parts to connect—just like when you connected the everywhere at once part to the working hard part.

5 **6** **7** Listening for a *partial understanding*, more *naming*, more "*Say more about that*." Notice how there's a bit of back-and-forth here, between naming and asking the reader to say more—this explains the two-sided arrow.

2 Again, jotting down exact words the reader says, without being too quick to interpret, will often lead to...

8 ... a *teaching point*. Here I state it clearly, *in transferable language that can apply to the next book, and the book after that*.

DAN: I have a thought. How would you like to do a project in this book where you look for connecting parts?

AMARI: That kind of sounds fun.

DAN: How about this. At the end of each chapter, go back and look for three connecting parts. What do you think?

AMARI: Yeah. Kind of sounds like a game, too.

DAN: So at the end of each chapter, go back and think, "What are three parts that connect?" You already found two, so you are already on the way. We can even color code it: three pink sticky notes for Chapter 1, three blue for Chapter 2... **9**

AMARI: *(Excitedly)* And three yellow for Chapter 3! So I already found one...where is it? Okay... *(Puts sticky note in book.)* **9**

DAN: Amari, doing this work is going to be very important for you. It's going to help you practice connecting parts that aren't so obvious how they go together. Just like you connected these parts because they were all about him working, but one of the examples doesn't even say he works. So you get to decide how they connect. Make sense? **10**

AMARI: It kind of does!

9 Here we negotiate *concrete*, *specific work to do in today's text* to practice and extend the teaching point—and Amari does a "try-it."

10 I end the conference by *articulating the teaching point*, *connecting it to future reading*.

Again, the steps of the conference are followed, roughly, in order—with some variation depending on the child and teacher. In Amari's conference, there was a lot of back-and-forth between naming and asking for elaboration ("Say more about that" are words to live by!). In another conference, there might be a more extended "try-it." Exactly how it goes depends on the direction of the conversation. Over time, a teacher can develop her own unique style of conferring, keeping those basic steps in mind.

Diagnostic Listening: What Did Amari Teach Us?

Though knowing content and structure are critical elements of conferring, in the end it all comes back to listening. Now that we've looked at the teacher moves in Amari's conference, let's consider what the student said and did—and what it teaches us about his comprehension.

First, Amari began with a retell of what he'd read so far ("Hank leads a couple of coyotes...Hank is a dog that works a lot and does lots of stuff...."). As basic as this may seem, Amari is determining importance; he specifically mentions leading the coyotes and then singles out an important character trait: "(he) works a lot and does lots of stuff." So, some prioritizing and also an awareness that it's important to get to know your characters early. Check.

Next, he shows he can infer beyond the literal ("So that tells me he does lots of work, because he's kind of complaining how he can't be everywhere at once."). Then when I ask Amari to find "other places... where you figured out something the author didn't exactly say," he quickly does so, showing a good ability to come up with text evidence. We've learned a fair amount already, but it's always a good idea to do as much research as possible before committing to a teaching point.

Finally, Amari goes metacognitive and talks about his thought process, no small thing for a second grader. "So when I first read this page, a while ago, I didn't understand about 'I can't be everywhere at once,' but then once I read that part, it told me." Bingo. He is synthesizing, connecting parts across a text—though before the conference he never realized he was doing it. This feels like the most sophisticated thing he's said or done in the conference, a zone-of-proximal-development moment. In other words, it's a partial understanding, something he is beginning to be able to do but isn't yet able to do consciously. It becomes the teaching point—"one of the things that readers have to do to read harder and harder books is decide which parts to connect"—and also the basis for his color-coding assignment.

Though knowing content and structure are critical elements of conferring, in the end it all comes back to listening.

One mantra to keep in mind is "Don't rush the research." Case in point: Early in Amari's conference, when he made the comment about how Hank "can't be everywhere at once," I thought my conference would focus on inference. After a bit more research—in this case, asking for additional examples—it became clear he wasn't inferring at all. The text actually *said* the dog was working hard. What Amari *was* doing was connecting parts. If I'd gone with my initial assessment, I would have missed the boat. The moral of the story is, you can always go back to your first idea—but by researching just a little longer, you may come up with something better.

This sort of diagnostic listening can seem at first like a magic trick ("The kid just talked about what the dog was doing, so how do you come up with all *that*?"). The truth is there are specific strategies—okay, tricks of the trade—that make it easier.

Teaching Point: Readers make decisions about which parts in a text to connect. Sometimes one part connects back to something from before and explains it.

Tricks of the Trade: Practical and Diagnostic Tips for Conferring With Readers

Interpret the Retell

Recently, while working in the Hendrick Hudson School District of Westchester, New York, I asked a fourth-grade student new to the class (and unaccustomed to conferring) to share what he was thinking about his book. "What do you mean, what am I *thinking*? I don't get it." The anxiety in his voice was palpable.

Many students don't know what we are talking about when we ask for their thoughts about books. And if we are to be honest, it's our fault as a profession that they don't. Children learn early on when a teacher asks them to talk about a book, it means one of two things: to answer a specific question posed by the teacher, or to summarize what they have read so far.

Clearly there are moments when asking a specific comprehension question is appropriate—and sometimes it makes sense to summarize. But, as Ellin Keene (2012) cautions, don't kid yourself you are teaching them anything—answering a comprehension question and retelling a text are assessment, not teaching. Moreover, neither are very engaging from the student's point of view. When most people are excited about a book, they don't call up a friend and tell them everything that happened in the last chapter—they share what it made them think about, or feel. Along the way, this usually involves recounting things from the text, but it's done in the service of expressing a thought. One of the objectives of a reading conference is to teach children how people actually talk about books in the world outside of school— as a way to express, explore, and grow their own thinking.

Back to that poor fourth grader in Westchester. After years of mostly retelling, it's sometimes necessary to reframe what it means to talk about text. One way is to plan whole-class lessons in which you model the difference between summarizing and expressing an idea (see page 53). In the meantime, many students will inevitably begin a conference by summarizing the book—whether asked to or not. When that happens, it falls to us to *interpret the retell*.

No, this is not fortune-telling. The truth is children summarize in very different ways; not all retells are created equal. Some may emphasize character feelings in a story ("She was really upset after the party, but her brother was acting all

> *One of the objectives of a reading conference is to teach children how people actually talk about books in the world outside of school—as a way to express, explore, and grow their own thinking.*

happy. And then the mom got suspicious!"). Others might recount details from a nonfiction text, one after another, but spend a long time on one especially important fact—prioritizing. Listening for what students tend to do (or not do) as they retell can provide a window into their thinking. It also provides an opportunity to make them aware of what they are doing as readers and nudge the conference into metacognitive territory. For example, in the case of the first student, a response could be, "Wow. I noticed as you were telling everything that happened in your book, you said a lot about the way characters were feeling. Is that something you usually do when you read? How does it help you understand the story better?" With the one-detail-after-another nonfiction student, we might observe, "You remembered a ton of information from your book! I noticed though that you spent a longer time talking about how lions hunt than some of the other facts. I'm guessing that you are the sort of reader who makes decisions about which facts are most important when you read nonfiction. Can you say more about that?"

Listening for what students tend to do (or not do) as they retell can give a window into their thinking. It also provides an opportunity to make them aware of what they are doing as readers.

Listening to how a child summarizes a text and matching it to a particular comprehension strategy is one way to learn about her as a reader. The following Interpreting the Retell chart shows some (not all) ways children tend to retell, matches them to one or more comprehension strategies, and suggests possible responses. There are also ideas for specific teaching points related to the comprehension strategy, and assignments students might do to practice. These suggestions are not meant to be scripts, but rather some (not all) possible ways to respond. Over time and with practice, a teacher will develop her own repertoire.

Professional Development/Grade-Meeting Activity: Together with colleagues, listen to recordings of students retelling. Match their summaries with particular comprehension strategies. (See the Content-of-Comprehension Cheat Sheet on page 165.) What parts of their retell show evidence of prioritizing? Did they reference earlier parts of the book while describing an event that happened later (synthesis)? What did they do best? What are some potential comprehension goals?

INTERPRETING THE RETELL

Did the student...	Comprehension strategy	You might say...	Teaching point	Assignment
...talk about characters' feelings?	Infer/Prioritize	• "How did you figure out she or he was feeling that way?" • "Do you pay attention to characters' feelings in other books? How does it help you understand the book?"	• Readers pay special attention to characters' feelings. • Readers notice how characters' feelings influence their actions/reactions.	• Find x number of places (e.g., in each chapter, from page 20 to page 50) that show characters' feelings, say how you know (sticky notes, T-chart, etc.). • A three-column chart: character/feelings/action
...describe the feeling of the story (e.g., depressing, funny, suspenseful, excited)?	Evoke Sensory/Emotional Images	• "I notice you are thinking about the way the book makes you feel. Can you find a part where the author made you feel that way?" • "Does the book always feel that way? Where is a place that feels different?"	• Readers pay attention to the mood of a book, and what authors do to make you feel that way. • Readers notice when the mood or feeling of a book changes.	• Find x number of places that illustrate the mood or feeling of a book (sticky notes, T-chart, etc.). • Keep track of parts where feelings change.
...emphasize or spend an especially long time on one part?	Determine Importance	• "When you read, do you pay special attention to the most important parts? How do you decide?"	• Readers make decisions about which parts of a text are most important.	• In each chapter/section, choose one most important part—say why it's important. (Possible extension: Choose a least important part!)
...connect two or more parts?	Synthesize	• "When you told me about your book, you talked about one part that went together with another part. Do you do that in other books, too? How does connecting parts help you to understand?"	• Readers pay special attention to parts that connect to other parts.	• A diagram with arrows that shows connecting parts; color-coded sticky notes to show connecting parts, transferred into a reading notebook with explanation.

Interpreting the Retell (cont.)

Did the student...	Comprehension strategy	You might say...	Teaching point	Assignment
...refer to a part from earlier in the book while explaining something that happened later?	**Synthesize/ Infer**	• "I noticed when you talked about this part, you mentioned something that happened before. When you read, do you stop and pay attention when you come to places that remind you of parts from earlier in the book? Tell me more about that."	• Readers stop and think when they come to places that connect back to things from earlier in the book.	• Color-coded sticky notes to show think-backward parts (and the part they connect back to); a diagram with arrows.
...mention something is confusing (e.g., "I don't know why she did that," "I'm not sure what happened then," etc.)?	**Monitor for Meaning**	• "You just did something really important—you realized there was a place where you didn't understand, and you stopped and thought about it. Can you tell me more about what you do when you come to places in books where you get confused?"	• Readers stop and think about places where they don't understand, think about what is confusing, and try to figure it out.	• Do a confusing parts study: Find x number of places where you don't understand, and jot a few words about exactly what is confusing. • Find x parts where you think the author wants you to be confused, and x parts where you don't understand.
...disagree with something in the book (e.g., what a character did, facts in an information book, etc.)?	**Question the Text**	• "It's so interesting how you come up with your own ideas about how the story should go/ which facts should be included. Do you do that in other books as well? Tell me more about that."	• Readers sometimes argue with a text, and compare what they would have done to the author's (or character's) decisions. • Readers sometimes compare the facts in an information book to what they know about the subject, and disagree or add to them in their mind.	• A T-chart comparing what the character did/said/thought/ felt to what you would have done. • A list of facts you disagree with (and why)—or of facts the author left out.
...comment on how something in the book reminds her of something she did or saw, or of another story?	**Access Prior Knowledge/ Make Connections**	• "I see you are thinking about parts in your book that remind you of things you've done/other stories you've read. How does connecting to your own life help you understand the book better?"	• Readers connect what they are reading to things in their own life, or things they know—and think about how these things can help them understand more fully.	• Sticky notes in places where you made a connection, and how it helped you understand. • A list of connections that helped you understand, and a list of connections that didn't.

Whole-Class Lesson With Sample Language

Teaching Point: What's the difference between summarizing and telling what you *think* about a book?

Materials:

Two prepared charts:
- One summarizing the current read-aloud, or another familiar text (Make it as dull as possible!)
- One expressing an idea about the same text (Make it as interesting as possible!)

Steps:

1. Sample language: "In our reading conferences, I've noticed that a lot of us begin by summarizing, telling everything that is happening in the book. Sometimes this can be helpful, especially if I haven't read it—but it's even more interesting to know what you are thinking. Let me show you the difference, and you can tell me which you think is more interesting."

2. Read aloud the summary chart in a boring voice, e.g., "Harry Potter is an 11-year-old boy who lives in England with a family called the Dursleys. They are mean to him. Harry doesn't know he is really a wizard."

3. Contrast the summary chart with the idea chart, e.g., "Harry Potter is supposed to be smart and strong, so it doesn't make sense that he allows himself to get pushed around by the Dursleys. He should stand up for himself."

4. Ask students which they think is more interesting, and why.

5. Have students try coming up with an idea statement, either about their independent book or the read-aloud. Sample language: "The second chart is definitely more interesting. In the first, I just told the facts of what happened in the story, but in the second, I told my own opinion about what was happening. Turn and talk to your neighbor right now and tell her/him an opinion you have about what is happening in your independent book."

6. Allow three to four minutes for turn and talk. Eavesdrop on conversations, and briefly report back on some of what you've heard.

7. End by repeating the teaching point, and why it's important. Sample language: "Readers, of course, need to understand what is happening, but just as importantly, they should always be coming up with their own ideas and opinions about their books. When we have reading conferences, I'll be very interested to hear your ideas and opinions!"

Possible Extension: Start a chart of *What Our Class Thinks About When We Think About Books*—naming ideas in general, transferable language that can apply to many books. For example, after showing the Harry Potter charts we might write: *Telling what we think the main character should do.* Add to the chart over the next several days as students come up with different types of ideas.

Adopt Kid Language

"The test of a first-rate intelligence," F. Scott Fitzgerald famously quipped back in 1936, "is the ability to hold two opposing ideas in the mind at the same time, and still retain the ability to function."

When we identify and name what a child is doing as a reader, there is a tension between honoring that student's thinking and taking away her sense of ownership. On one hand, it is our job to introduce students to academic vocabulary, so they learn the way readers in the world talk about books. On another hand, one of the primary goals in a conference is for the student to feel like the ideas being explored come from her.

One way to straddle this seeming contradiction is, whenever possible, adapt the student's own words to describe the comprehension strategy she is beginning to approximate.

As an example, let's look at part of a conference with fourth grader Nico about his nonfiction book *Frogs, Toads, and Turtles*.

DAN: You chose this page as one of your favorites in the book, right?

NICO: Yeah.

DAN: What made this page so interesting?

NICO: The interesting part is I didn't know frogs know how to play dead. And frogs can swim ten times faster than the fastest swimmer in the world!

DAN: I see that sentence right there—that is a really cool fact. What was so interesting about that fact for you?

NICO: When I just started reading, I read the whole thing, then I did a song on it.

DAN: What kind of a song?

NICO: Do you want me to sing it? *(Sings.)* "A frog can swim—da-da-da-duh—ten times faster—than the fastest swimmer in the who-ole world—da-da-da-dow!"

Nico sings his response to an interesting fact about frogs in our virtual reading conference.

DAN: That's so great! I love music myself, too. What about that sentence inspired you to write a song?

NICO: I just read it many times, and then... I make a song in my head.

DAN: I'm interested in one thing you said—you said you read that sentence a couple of times. Tell me about that—what made you read it more than once?

NICO: I just saw the first one, I stared at the first sentence, I stared at that one and said, "Whoa!"

DAN: So that was a "Whoa!" sentence for you.... On this page, were there any other sentences that were "Whoa" sentences?

Teaching Point: Readers make decisions about facts that are most important ("Whoa!" facts) and those that are less important ("boring" facts).

There are a few instructional moves worth highlighting in this exchange. First, asking Nico to talk about a concrete part in the book got him to describe his thinking more specifically, rather than just speaking in generalities (more on this later). Second, allowing him to be playful (this is the only conference I've ever done where a kid burst into song!) made him comfortable enough to take chances expressing his thinking; metacognition, after all, doesn't come easily to most eight-year-olds.

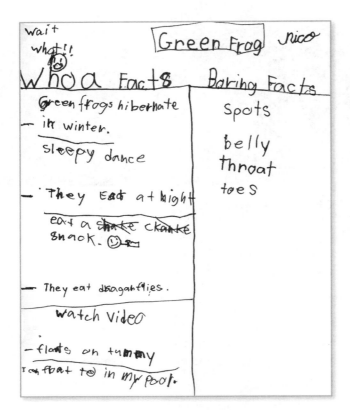

Green Frog — Nico

Whoa Facts	Boring Facts
Green frogs hibernate in winter.	spots
sleepy dance	belly
They Eat at night	throat
eat a snake chanke snack.	toes
They eat dragonflies.	
watch video	
floats on tummy	
float in my pool.	

wait what!!

Use Conversational Moves to Help Students Come Up With Their Own Ideas

When asked to share their thinking about a book, some kids rise to the occasion and go on at length. Others answer monosyllabically ("It's good," "It's funny") or not at all. Especially when they are used to responding to teacher prompts that tell them what to think about ("What are the character traits of ____?" "How would you describe the lesson of the story?" "Which facts are most important?"), students often have a hard time coming up with ideas of their own.

The good news is that over time, with repeated practice and opportunities to hear what other students in the class are thinking, most young readers—even those initially resistant—get better at expressing their individual thoughts and feelings about books. In the meantime, it's helpful to have some go-to strategies to help children come up with their own ideas.

Last, rather than explaining to Nico what he was doing was *prioritizing*, or *determining importance* by highlighting the frog swimming fact, I purposely adopted his language and named it as a "Whoa" fact. He smiled at this acknowledgment, and later in the conference when I asked if he was the sort of reader who paid special attention to "Whoa" facts, he was excited to do an assignment contrasting the "Whoa" with the boring. (As a special bonus, he included what each "Whoa" fact would inspire him to do.)

Consider the Opposite

My two daughters, Sonia and Kiri, had very different approaches to school when they were growing up.

At a memorable parent-teacher conference evening when she was in middle school, several of Sonia's teachers made slightly differing versions of the same comment: "She's very good when the expectation is to come up with your own parameters, and usually takes a leadership role in group projects. But there's a problem when an assignment has to be done a certain way—she always comes back and says she thought of a different way to do it." (As a rebellious soul, my heart warmed hearing this "problem.")

Kiri, on the other hand, practically had a nervous breakdown whenever instructions for an assignment felt open-ended. Many a tear-filled night was spent reassuring her that, really, the teacher wanted *her* to come up with her own way. "No!" she would protest in a panicky voice. "How am I *supposed* to do it?" (Her anxiety was heartbreaking, especially since when pressed, she came up with great ideas!)

This contrast in personality type (which, let's face it, exists in adults as well) is especially evident in children. As noted in an earlier chapter, kids are typically concrete thinkers. Many have difficulty being flexible in their thinking even under the best of circumstances, and the tendency is exacerbated when they are worried about "getting it right." As Dr. Justin Coulson (2019) points out, "negative emotions shut our thinking down. And (when) kids are having that big emotion...their brain literally starts to operate in fight/flight mode."

Sometimes when a teacher asks a student to elaborate on her ideas, it can feel like a correction—an indirect message that the first thing she said wasn't good enough. One way to coax deeper thinking from children is to encourage them to "shift perspective...help them see things from different views so they see their perspective isn't the only one." (Coulson again.) The trick is to do this in such a way that it sounds like an invitation rather than a criticism.

Asking students to *consider the opposite* of whatever they are saying can be freeing—and easier to wrap their heads around than digging deeper into just one idea. For example, if a child says her book is depressing, we might ask, "Is it ever *not* depressing?" When a student says the main character is brave, we might ask if there are any places in the book where she is not brave. Or mean. Or generous.

I've found this move to be especially helpful in getting reluctant talkers to open up. For whatever reason, considering the opposite seems less risky than having to wrack their brains for further evidence of what they've already said. And ironically, turning their initial observations around often results in readers thinking more deeply about the idea they had in the first place.

To illustrate this point, here is a partial transcript of a conference with fifth grader Kira as she talks about her independent reading, *My Side of the Mountain*.

DAN: I hear you are the kind of reader that likes to make connections to her reading. Can you tell me a little about that?

KIRA: Since my family, we do a lot, we travel a lot of places, so we've done a lot of things. So if I read a sentence that I like, then I think, well, I've done this before.

DAN: So the kinds of connections you make are to things you've done?

KIRA: Yeah.

DAN: I get it. Can you give me an example of that, in this book?

KIRA: Well, he goes traveling on a mountain and I remember when I was little, I used to like to climb mountains.

DAN: I have kind of a hard question. How does connecting to that help you understand the book better?

KIRA: It helps me understand 'cause maybe I'll know how they are feeling, if they don't explain it—because I know how I was feeling. So it'll help me.

DAN: Now I have another hard question. There are some places where you make a connection and it helps you understand. Are there any places where you make a connection, and it *doesn't* help you understand?

KIRA: *(Pauses.)* Well, if there was a favorite kind of food that wouldn't help me, because it doesn't really help explain the story at all.

From here I asked her to go into the book and find examples of both types of connections—again, talking off something concrete. She quickly came up with one of each. (*Helpful: What it feels like to climb a mountain. Not helpful: Went to the library*.) We agreed that sometimes connections can help you make sense of a book, but at times they can just be distracting. (*Teaching point: Readers make decisions about which personal connections help them understand, and which are distracting*.) Kira was excited to go off and find more examples, creating a two-column chart of Helpful and Not Helpful connections.

Teaching Point: Readers make decisions about which personal connections help them understand, and which are distracting.

HELPFUL Mrs.Stacy's class

- In the book he climbed a mountain and once I have climbed a mountain too. This is helpful because it helps me understand how he might be feeling since I have done it too.
- He has a connection with animals and so do I! (my cats) This is helpful because maybe he is an animal kind of person, so he will be kind to future animals in the book.
- He went to the library and so have I! This is helpful because maybe that means he likes to read and that he is knowlegable.
- He likes to play outside, so do I! This is helpfull because maybe he likes the outdoors and knows a lot about it.
- He is friendly, so am I! This is helpful because he will be helpful and respectfull to the envirment.

NOT HELPFUL

- He has been in a forest before and so have I! This isn't helpful because it does not tell any extra details in MY OPINION!
- His father owns a farm and I remember going to a farm. Not helpful because it does not explain anything about the story.
- He saw a bird and I have seen a bird before. It does not explain any extra details.
- He made a tree fort and so have I! This isn't helpful because again no extra details.
- He has a pet, so do I. This isn't because it doesn't give extra clues.

Before this conference, it never occurred to Kira that not all personal connections help a reader to understand. Considering the opposite helped her dig deeper into the idea of connections in general, and her own connections in particular. In addition, the act of writing provided an opportunity for reflection. Case in point, it's interesting to note that after thinking about it further, she decided the library was a helpful connection after all!

If a Child Says...	Consider the Opposite!
The book is: • depressing • funny • filled with action • exciting • confusing • unrealistic • surprising • boring	Is it: • ever not depressing (e.g., happy, funny, etc.)? • ever serious? • filled with action always, or are some parts calm? • ever not exciting? • ever not confusing? • unrealistic all through, or are any parts true to life? • ever not surprising? • ever interesting?
A character is: • nice • bad • smart • sad • brave	Is he/she/they ever: • not so nice? • good? • not so smart? • happy? • scared?

Find a Part

I've been reading books with my friend John Tintori for more than 20 years. Our two-person book club began at a dinner party when, after a couple glasses of bourbon, we challenged each other to read Dostoyevsky's *The Brothers Karamazov*. (Me: "That book is so long, no one would ever read it unless someone forced them." John: "Okay, I'm going to force you." Me: "Oh yeah? I'm going to force *you*.") We've continued to read very long classics and complex, modern literary fiction, and the conversations (often fueled by a glass or two) sometimes veer into the abstract. I look forward to our meetings, where we discuss (for example) how Tolstoy's morality gets in the way of his storytelling, or the way Chimamanda Ngozi Adichie raises questions about American cultural norms. Sometimes when I recount these conversations to my partner, Suzy, she gets impatient. "Don't you guys ever just talk about what *happens* in the book?"

Asking a child to tell what she is thinking or feeling about a book can be, well, not very specific. Many will respond with those dreaded monosyllabic utterances, and then wait hopefully for the teacher to come to the rescue.

Once again, children are concrete thinkers and tend to do better when talking about something tangible. Often the students who are least forthcoming in conferences open up and surprise us when asked to *find an example* of something they've noticed. This means choosing an actual page or passage in the book. It doesn't have to be something wildly sophisticated—just about anything will do. When a second grader responds to, "What are you thinking?" with a simple, "Good," we might ask her to find a "good" part to show what she means. If a fourth grader says he likes it because it's exciting, our next question might be, "Can you show me an exciting part?"

Not surprisingly, this simple move usually brings forth ideas in a way that asking in the abstract does not. A close look at Amari's conference on pages 43–46 shows that at first, his only comment is, "So far I know that Hank is a dog that works a lot and does lots of stuff. That's pretty much all I know." But when I asked him to find a part in the text, he went on to make inferences ("Can't be everywhere at once" means he's working hard); discuss personal experiences (siblings bossing him around); and think about how parts connected ("At first I thought...but then I read..."). Kira (p. 58) started off her conference with a generic explanation of why she made personal connections. After going into the text, she began to think (and talk) more deeply about when those connections were and weren't helpful.

It might be tempting for the teacher to choose an interesting passage ahead of time to discuss. After all, wouldn't that save time? It's important to note that in each of these cases, the student, not the teacher, chose the part to talk about. For a child to feel ownership—like the idea came from *her*—it is no small thing to be the one who gets to flip through the pages and *find a part*. Interestingly, though I've experienced many students saying, "I don't know," when asked to express a thought, I've never had one hesitate to look for a page in a book.

This move invites deeper thinking with just about any student, not just the most struggling or reluctant readers. A look at this partial transcript of middle school teacher Anna Schlosser's conference with seventh grader Aaliyah at the American School of the Hague shows how going into the text pushed an engaged, higher-level reader even further.

ANNA: Hi, Aaliyah. Tell me about the book you're reading.

AALIYAH: I'm rereading *Anne of Windy Poplars*. I wanted to finish it
            quickly, for the Book Examination, so I rushed through the
            last few chapters. But I don't like this book at all.

ANNA: What do you not like about it?

AALIYAH: Well, it doesn't really have a climax, if you know what I mean.
            It's just more like, about her life. This is the fourth book of
            the Anne of Green Gables series, and there's eight books.
            And I have this thing that's probably bad, like I can't just stop
            reading a series of books. Like I have to finish it, even if I don't
            like it, which is bad. And the third book was really good, and
            this one is—ugh....

ANNA: So it's dragging. It's kind of dull, and there's no climax,
            and we've been talking a lot about climax as we write our
            short stories. So, is there ever a part in that book where it's
            not boring? Can you turn to a page that you found more
            interesting, or exciting?

Up until now, Aaliyah is chatty enough—but not very specific in discussing her
thinking. Anna asks her to *consider the opposite*, and also go back into the text
to find an example. And then...

AALIYAH: Oh! Probably the one that I was reading right now. *(She flips
            to the page in the book.)*

ANNA: Talk to me about why this part is exciting to you.

AALIYAH: There's this girl—they also throw in random characters, it's
            hard to keep up with—but there's a girl and a boy and they've
            always loved each other. But they never did anything about
            it, because the girl's dad hated him, that's what it looked like.
            And they ended up getting married secretly, in a rush, and
            she didn't want to, because her dad would hate her, and blah
            blah blah. And then Anne had to go to her dad and break
            the news. But the dad didn't even care, he was happy about
            it. It was just like a strategy, 'cause that family was known
            for getting things that they couldn't get. And so it's kind of

exciting because she thinks it's going to be terrible and he's going to have a terrible temper and stuff, and he's just happy.

ANNA: So are you saying it's exciting because there's a conflict between the characters that's developing?

AALIYAH: Yeah.

ANNA: Can you say a little bit more about this conflict—not what's happening in the conflict, but why it's interesting? What is it about the way the author is telling you the story of this conflict that you find interesting?

AALIYAH: Probably because they build up to what you think would happen. Like they tell you how the dad is always mad. Whenever something goes a certain way that he doesn't like, he has really bad reactions. So you get anxious for Anne, thinking the dad is going to be really mean and stuff—and then it doesn't happen at all.

Once talking about a specific passage in the text, Aaliyah goes deep. With Anna's encouragement ("Say more about this"), she not only recounts relevant details to back up her thinking, but goes on to reflect on how the author made things interesting ("they build up to what you think would happen...So you get anxious... and then it doesn't happen at all."). Pretty heady stuff, for a 12-year-old. But at the beginning of the conference, all she did was talk in a general way about how boring it was.

Anna and Aaliyah agreed that an interesting follow-up assignment would be to look for other places where the author sets you up to expect one thing, and then surprises you. ("That would be a way to make it more interesting," Anna suggests, acknowledging Aaliyah's initial complaint.) So the teaching point (*Readers pay special attention to places where authors make us expect one thing, but then do another*), apart from being a pretty sophisticated way to look at a story, is connected to a purpose that comes from the child.

Teaching Point: Readers pay special attention to places where authors make us expect one thing, but then do another.

> **Tip: "Find a Part," Virtually or in Person:** This book was written during the COVID-19 pandemic, when most conferences took place virtually. I found it helpful while conferring on Zoom to ask students to think ahead about a page or passage they wanted to talk about, take a screenshot, and look at it together at the start of the conversation. Once things got back to normal, several teachers reported that this ritual—letting students know the day before that their conference was coming up, and thinking ahead about a page to talk about—made conferences feel more focused, and provided a natural starting point.

Keeping Track: Note-Taking and Record-Keeping

As Ralph Fletcher puts it, conferences are "an ongoing conversation that will last all year." But none of us can realistically hope to remember from one week to the next (let alone from month to month) exactly what we talked about with every child. Moreover, if each new conference is approached as *tabula rasa*—a completely new lesson from the one before—we make it more difficult for both ourselves and our students. From the young reader's point of view, it is harder to make connections and build on new strategies. From the adult's perspective, having to start from scratch each time is stressful, to say the least.

Though conferring is by definition reactive teaching, this doesn't mean we don't plan ahead. Developing a record-keeping system is critical for creating long-term comprehension goals, and for thinking in advance about where to go in the next conference. It can also help with finding an instructional direction for a single conference; sometimes in the act of jotting down memorable phrases from a student, a teaching point becomes apparent. (Think back to Amari's conference on pages 43–46. In my notes, I jotted down "When I first read this page, I didn't understand...but then once I read that part...." When I saw those words, I thought "bingo"—connecting parts, or synthesis.)

Taking notes during a conference may be challenging at first. Some of us find it difficult to respond to a student while also recording what she is saying. Whether we use a more formal record-keeping form (see page 171) or develop our own personal shorthand, it is helpful to narrow note-taking down to just what's essential. In *Reading Projects Reimagined* (2015), I suggest:

Record the:

- key words/phrases used by the student
- teaching point
- assignment
- due date

Some of the reasons for this are logistical. At the very least, a teacher needs to remember assignments and due dates. Since the first part of the conference relies heavily on asking students to *say more* about specific things, it's critical to get down exact words and phrases. Nothing signals careful listening better or makes children feel more important than when their teacher says their actual words back to them.

Once the conference is over (but still fresh in your head), some teachers also find it useful to quickly jot down ideas for next steps. Whether or not we end up using those ideas in the next conference, having a set of possible directions can ease the anxiety of coming up with something completely new each time. And if we don't go there in the next conference, there's always the one after that.

Here as an example are the notes from Amari's conference on pages 43–46. Except for the "Possible next steps" (and fixing a few typos), they are exactly as I took them during the actual conference, warts and all. Included are several actual quotes from Amari, as well as diagnostic thoughts that occurred to me along the way. Perhaps most importantly, I was careful to record the teaching point in transferable language that could apply to other books, separate from the specific assignment. Looking this over before my next meeting with Amari allowed me to begin the next conference by asking him, "How is it going choosing which parts to connect in *this* book?"

Amari—Book: *Hank the Cowdog*—"Hank is a dog that works a lot"—cites text evidence: Can't be everywhere at once, "shows he works a lot"—inference—also connects to own life—I ask for another inference part, he reads "works a lot"—says it!—synthesis, connecting parts, tho he didn't name it himself—can he do across longer text?—"When I first read this page, I didn't understand…but then once I read that part…" Mentions second part helped him understand earlier part re: working hard—gets thinking changes as we read (monitor for mng!)

T.P.—Rdrs. need to know which parts to connect—sometimes one part connects BACK to something from before and explains it

- Assignment—Find three connecting parts for each of the first three chaps, color code

Possible next steps:

- Connecting parts and what it made you think about (___ + ___ = My idea) (Synth/inference)
- Look for "At first I didn't understand, but then" parts (Monitor for Mng)
- Parts that *don't* connect (M for M)

Keith Stanulis, a fifth-grade teacher at Hong Kong International School, sets up his conferring notes in chart form. In addition to noting the assignment's due date, he adds in a progress update once it has been turned in.

NAME	DATE	NOTES	PROJECT
CLAUDIA Z	Jan 23	Geek Girl series, 5th one, RF. College girls, like the friendship challenges the girls face. Likes how the girls have to work together to solve their problems. Harriet, can relate to the most. Sometimes the parents give way too much freedom to the girls. Not very realistic.	Keeping track of places in the story where "things don't add up." For example, the author has the parents allowing the girls to go off to London at a moment's notice. Keep a chart of at least 4 places where the author has places where you don' t believe parts of the story are realistic. Today: Monday Jan 23 Due: Fri. Feb 10th **Progress Update:** Feb. 8 Ck-in: Finished Geek Girls #5 and had one event recorded. We listed 3 more events to which Claudia connecte and she was ready to finish the chart today. Claudia did not do the "things don't add up" chart but rather a "big events to which the reader can connect" chart. She started Lily Alone (she read a long time ago) but able to better understand it now. She will make another big event/ personal connection chart for Lily Alone but will add a character traits + example chart too.

NAME	DATE	NOTES	PROJECT
DANIEL Y	Jan 19	Number the Stars, HF, don't really read that much, every other day, enjoyed the Once series, loves HF. Number the Stars, wondering when Denmark will help, likes to look for who's going to save the day, makes the book more interesting, paying close attention to the dad, looking to see if he turns out to be a good or bad guy. Looking at the quotes of character, thinking about if I can trust the dad	Create a doc or visual that helps track evidence to help you determine if you can trust the dad. Based on what he says and does in the story, you'll reflect on whether or not this is increasing or decreasing your trust meter. **Progress Update:** Feb. 10th Completed the document. Expected him to say more things in the story, but he didn't. He discovered that some things the dad said were his true feelings and some things were kind of fishy. The project helped him analyze what the characters are doing in the story.

Jesse Meyer, Keith's colleague at HKIS, keeps notes on a more elaborate spreadsheet. Note how he accentuates the positive, adding in a column for student strengths and clearly articulating the teaching point. Each student gets her own tab in the notes file as well, making it easier to track growth over time and connect one conference to another.

Reading Conference Note-Taking Form

Name	Book Title and Author	Strengths	Teaching Point	Project Description	Due Date
Kat	Aru Shah and the End of Time	• Recognized a pattern in her previous project that led to a new project. • Allowed her project to change her thinking about the characters' relationship. • Kat is a very analytic thinker who reads above grade level.	Readers notice how events in a story change the relationships between characters.	pg# - event - how Boo and Aru's relationship evolves (or changes)	11/1
Kat	The Explorer	• Compared two characters to each other and other characters at the start and end of the book. • Kept meticulous notes and was able to analyze for patterns.	Great readers compare and contrast different characters and the same character at the start and the end of the book.	Focus the notices and wonders on comparing and contrasting characters in preparation for writing an essay.	1/14
Kat	The Explorer	• Asked for a conference in order to meet deadline • Neat, orderly work • Kept evidence that included awesome quotes from the text.	Write a paragraph based on the project.		1/14

Go to page 169 and scholastic.com/RadicalListeningResources for a reproducible/ downloadable version of this form.

Professional Development/Grade-Meeting Activity: Record or videotape reading conferences. Watch them with colleagues. Take notes for each conference as though it were your own. Compare notes. Specifically, which phrases of the child did you write down? What did they tell you about the child's comprehension? Remember, there are no right or wrong answers!

Reading Conference Tracking Sheet

Name: Sharonda	Class: 602	Date: 10/24/21

Pre-Conference Notes

- 1st conference, new 6th grader
- observed in first few days that she is a reader, asked for access to class library
- enjoys writing original stories; writes during down time
- often asks for spelling help while story writing; words usually suggest dark topics in her writing (may be interested in the same in novels)
- likes fantasy; first chose then abandoned Chronicles of Narnia
- As we examine characterization, shows clear understanding of literary elements/character types

Conference Structure:

- Listen
- Ask reader to say more on selected topic/idea
- Jot down notes
- Name skill (teaching point)
- Create assignment
- Review teaching point

Text Title: Twelve Minutes to Midnight by Christopher Edge

Conference Notes

- Chose novel because of interesting cover, "…brings chaos closer"
- early in the novel, pages into the first chapter
- still figuring out where the story is going
- hasn't met the protagonist yet
- has figured out the protagonist is Penelope, a "feisty 15-year-old orphan"
- Montgomery Flinch — character is introduced
- Flinch is a popular story writer
- He reads to his audience (book reading)
- Penelope seems to like him
- When he greets audience, they say, "Yeah, Mr. Flinch!" (page 2)
- Penelope may be one of his fans, strong feeling (tell me more)
- A little confused, but feels like a connection between the two

Name Skill/Strategy (Teaching Point):
Making inferences about characters and finding supportive evidence

Assignment:
Create a character trait and evidence chart. One on Penelope and another on Montgomery Flinch.

Due Date: 10/21/21

Next Steps:

Character Interaction — examining the interaction between Penelope and Montgomery Flinch

(Note to self: Discussed doing this now, but decided to focus on each character first, then build to how they interact. Hoping she discovers that Penelope is Montgomery.)

Sonya Simpson, a teacher at Restoration Academy Middle School in Bedford-Stuyvesant, Brooklyn, devised this tracking sheet.

Sonya Simpson, a teacher at Restoration Academy Middle School in Bedford-Stuyvesant, Brooklyn, devised this tracking sheet. See page 170 and scholastic.com/RadicalListeningResources for a blank, reproducible version.

Reading Conference Record-Keeping Form

Name: Kira   **Class:** 5R

Date: 11/10   **Book:** My Side of the Mountain   **Page:**

What We Talked About	Strategy Taught by Teacher	What Students Will Work On
Personal connections: K: "When I read some sentences, I think that I've done this!" How does it help? K: "I kind of know how the character was feeling." When does it not help? The connection to food doesn't help K understand the story.	Readers make decisions re: which personal connections help them understand the story and which are just distractions.	Find 5 helpful and 5 not-so helpful connections, say why

Date: 11/18   **Book:** Because of Winn-Dixie   **Page:**

What We Talked About	Strategy Taught by Teacher	What Students Will Work On
Helpful/not helpful connections: K: "Sometimes I think something is helpful at first but then not—and vice versa." Example: grocery store K: "Understand feelings— then I know why characters do things."	Often a character's strong feelings help explain the character's actions. Readers connect feelings to character's actions. (Synth/Cause & Effect)	2-column chart with arrows: Feelings That Lead to Actions (6 ex, Ch. 1–6)

Date: **Book:**   **Page:**

What We Talked About	Strategy Taught by Teacher	What Students Will Work On

Here are my notes from Kira's conference (p. 58), as well as our conference the following week. Notice how referencing the strategy taught on 11/10 (recorded on the record-keeping form) led to a new teaching point on 11/18. See page 171 and scholastic.com/RadicalListeningResources for a blank, reproducible version.

Sharing and Feedback

Sharing the Work of Reading Conferences

Traditionally, reading comprehension is taught with a "right answer" mentality. Students are tested on their ability to identify a main idea and back it up with text evidence. But any text worth reading contains *many* ideas—and that's just when we consider the words on the page. In addition, the unique perspective of an individual reader can bring new meaning still to a text. A Latinx fifth grader living near the border of Mexico is likely to have different ideas about Pam Muñoz Ryan's *Becoming Naomi Leon* than an upper-middle-class White kid. Similarly, a third grader from Doha will probably take away different ideas when reading a National Geographic World book about deserts than the same-age student from a classroom in New Jersey.

It makes sense that when we value (and celebrate!) the multiple perspectives and ideas in our class, students are more likely to become flexible thinkers who value (and respect!) other points of view. By creating regular routines for students to share the thinking that comes out of their individual reading conferences, we promote a vision of equity in the classroom. Since this work grows out of an individual child's thinking, sharing it regularly sends the important message that everyone in the class has ideas worth considering—the "democracy of reading" Philip Pullman talks about.

> "As a passionate believer in the democracy of reading, I don't think it's the task of the author of a book to tell the reader what it means. The meaning of a story emerges in the meeting between the words on the page and the thoughts in the reader's mind. So when people ask me what I meant by this story, or what was the message I was trying to convey in that one, I have to explain that I'm not going to explain. Anyway, I'm not in the message business; I'm in the 'Once upon a time' business."
>
> —PHILIP PULLMAN

And, not for nothing, stressing the notion that there are different ways to look at a text is truer to the nature of reading than prioritizing one "main" idea.

There are many ways to integrate the sharing of individual conference work into the routines of a reading classroom. In a traditional reading workshop setting, the 5- to 10-minute share time at the end of a period can be alternately about "who tried what was modeled in today's mini-lesson" and "let's look at some of the interesting individual thinking going on in our class." Asking students ahead of time to share what they discussed at a conference, and even giving them a moment to practice with a friend beforehand, will help these sessions feel more focused.

Many teachers find it helpful to ask students who are *not* sharing to consider, as they listen to their classmates, which conferring lessons might be useful in their own work. Franco Rodriguez, a third-grade teacher at Shen Wai International School in Shenzhen, China, recounts:

> "After a nice conference with Phil on his nonfiction reading, I asked him if he'd like to share. He didn't. But he was very willing to let *me* share our conference with the class. I told them he was reading an informational text about firefighters, and working on writing a good summary. I communicated to the class that he found a way to determine importance by labeling some facts as 'needed' and some facts as 'not needed' in his summary, and that this is what readers do! I invited students to try his new strategy, and I saw a gleam in Phil's eye I'd never seen from him during reading class. I mean, how could he have done something so good that the teacher is telling other students to try what he did?! It was beautiful."

> "And, that's just what another student did. Mary turned to him during our next independent reading time to ask him how to do his strategy. And Phil taught Mary. It was adorable. She then in turn used his strategy. And after that, we shared *her* experience. From them, it snowballed. At least half of the class was using Phil's strategy."

> "From that point on, strategies were kept in a central place in our classroom for students to refer to, and that they did! We had waves of students using the same strategies. What came of it was a supportive, caring, and eager classroom environment. We were on our way...chills!"

Put bluntly, the truth is that anything in teaching succeeds or fails in direct proportion to how big a deal we make of it. If you are the only person to see and discuss students' individual conference work, it's a safe bet it will die in the water. On the other hand, when students get the idea that some of the work in reading class comes from the teacher, but some of it comes from *them*, the level of engagement rises exponentially. To this end, in addition to regular time for sharing, it's helpful to create physical spaces in the classroom—or virtually—where children can see and be inspired by each other's individual conference work. These may take the form of bulletin board displays or shared documents in cyberspace.

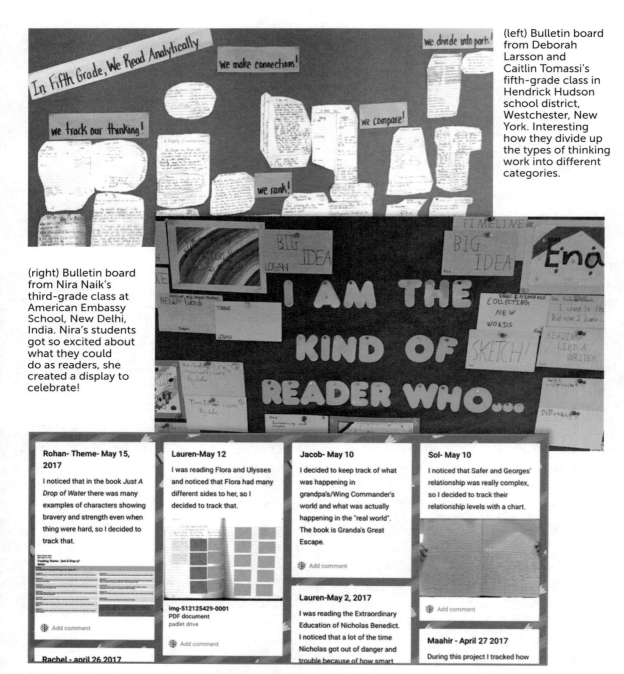

(left) Bulletin board from Deborah Larsson and Caitlin Tomassi's fifth-grade class in Hendrick Hudson school district, Westchester, New York. Interesting how they divide up the types of thinking work into different categories.

In Fifth Grade, We Read Analytically

we make connections!

we divide into parts!

we track our thinking!

we compare!

we rank!

(right) Bulletin board from Nira Naik's third-grade class at American Embassy School, New Delhi, India. Nira's students got so excited about what they could do as readers, she created a display to celebrate!

TIMELINE

BIG IDEA

BIG IDEA

Ena

COLLECTING NEW WORDS

SKETCH!

READING LIKE A WRITER

I AM THE KIND OF READER WHO...

Rohan- Theme- May 15, 2017

I noticed that in the book *Just A Drop of Water* there was many examples of characters showing bravery and strength even when thing were hard, so I decided to track that.

Add comment

Rachel - april 26 2017

Lauren-May 12

I was reading Flora and Ulysses and noticed that Flora had many different sides to her, so I decided to track that.

img-512125429-0001
PDF document
padlet drive

Add comment

Jacob- May 10

I decided to keep track of what was happening in grandpa's/Wing Commander's world and what was actually happening in the "real world". The book is Granda's Great Escape.

Add comment

Lauren-May 2, 2017

I was reading the Extraordinary Education of Nicholas Benedict. I noticed that a lot of the time Nicholas got out of danger and trouble because of how smart

Sol- May 10

I noticed that Safer and Georges' relationship was really complex, so I decided to track their relationship levels with a chart.

Add comment

Maahir - April 27 2017

During this project I tracked how

(above) A shared virtual space set up by Keith Stanulis for his fifth graders at Hong Kong International School to share their individual reading conference assignments. Note the additional spaces below each assignment for children to comment on one another's work.

> I am focusing on how different things can lead to changes in the book. I am mainly looking how Plot, character action, and internal thinking can all have a Pattern in the book.

Maureen Ienuso, a middle school teacher at Mt. Zaagkam School in Papua, Indonesia, has students post their conferring assignments publicly on sticky notes and share when finished. Sixth grader Nikki was interested in the relationship between plot events, character actions, and internal thinking in Deborah Ellis's *The Breadwinner*. When she shared with the class, Nikki reflected, "I realized that internal thinking almost never comes first. Something in the plot has to happen or the character needs to do something for internal thinking to build."

Example 1:

Plot event:	Character Actions:	Internal thinking
Parvana's Father is arrested by the Taliban. They barged into the apartment and dragged her father out.	Parvana descises as a boy in order to hide her female Identity because its easier that way	At first Parvana got Upset because she had to cut her hair etc. but she later got used to it.

Example 2 -

Character Actions	Plot events	Internal thinking
Parvana and Shauzia went to this arena to sell goods.	The taliban were executing people right infant of many.	They thought everything was normal but this couldve scared them forever

Example 3 -

Character Actions	Plot events	Internal Thinking
Parvana decided to work and read letters like her Father	A Taliban man told Parvana his story and said to read his letter,	This mader her the think that Taliban are also Just people Who have feelings

Example 4s

Plot events	internal thinking	Char. actions
Parvana was out one day and saw this hurt girl	She thoght about her and was empathetic.	She helped the girl (home) and brought her home and took care of her

Providing Opportunities for Feedback and Reflection

It's important for students to feel their conference work is "low stakes"—a safe place where they are free to take chances and explore new ideas without being graded. But when children see their *other* work returned with teacher comments, they may feel conference assignments are less important. Andrea Holck, a middle school teacher who had recently moved from a school in Istanbul to Northern California, had this to say when I asked for her thoughts on providing feedback to students about their reading conferences:

> "Honestly, I don't like the idea of using rubrics, checklists, and so on, for reading conference work since what I think is so beautiful about them is their ability to transcend all that 'administrivial' stuff we like to append to student work. (I'm coming out of a frustrating meeting on said appendages and am currently frustrated with all such business.)"

It's important for students to feel their conference work is "low stakes"—a safe place where they are free to take chances and explore new ideas without being graded.

> "What I have done, and continue to do, is have a running log of each student's work. For a conference, we write the description together, which includes the goals stated clearly, and then I add my feedback to the student into that note, so at the next conference we can look at where we were going to push and integrate that into our next work. I do only narrative feedback. Because I space projects out so that I'm never getting more than four in one day, I find it manageable to give substantive feedback on each project. I respond totally freely, but always make sure to indicate something to push next time, so we're always building."

> "That's probably a frustrating answer, or maybe a delightful one, depending on your current relationship to assessment tools. More and more, especially since coming back to the United States, I find myself having a lot more confidence in my own ability to give the right feedback to a child, drawing on everything I know about him or her and what he or she is trying to do, and that could never be captured in a rubric, especially given the nature of individualized projects."

Other teachers and administrators feel if valuable teaching time is being spent on reading conferences, the students' work should be assessed in a more formal way. Since most assignments focus on comprehension rather than polished writing, it's important that the criteria for assessment reflect the work. In other words, it should be about the quality of thinking, and not looked at in the same way as a revised and edited assignment. Here's an example of an eighth-grade rubric created by the ELA teachers at Restoration Academy in Brooklyn, assessing students' ability to reference text evidence.

8th GRADE READING CONFERENCE RUBRIC				
R.I. Standard 8.1	Level 1	Level 2	Level 3	Level 4
Cite the textual evidence that most strongly supports an analysis of what the text says explicitly as well as inferences drawn from the text.	• May refer to the text but not to any specific section; may discuss the topic with no reference to the text. • May refer only to one or two parts of the text without an attempt to synthesize them; may rely solely on explicit facts and details.	• May cite evidence that is somewhat connected to an analysis or may paraphrase from the text to support a theory about the text. • Summarizes key points in the text that are explicitly stated; may rely mostly on explicit information and may not analyze the development of these points.	• Cites textual evidence that is clearly supportive of an analysis of the text. • Analyzes the development of central ideas in the text, based on explicit and implicit messages and information.	• Accurately cites several pieces of textual evidence that clearly support an analysis of the text. • Develops a sophisticated analysis of the text's explicit and implicit messages and how those messages are communicated through key ideas and details.

Whether evaluative or formative, it's important to provide regular feedback on conferring work, so students know it counts. As important, if they are to see that the work is, as Andrea put it, "always building," children should have opportunities to reflect on it themselves. It is a good idea to keep a collection of students' conferring assignments and ask them periodically to look back at their own growth. Jesse Meyer at Hong Kong International School has his upper-elementary students fill out a reflection sheet about their conference work toward the end of the year, and meets with each one to discuss her progress.

Reading Conference Reflection Sheet

Name:	Georgia	Date:

Book Title:	Stanford Wong Flunks Big-Time	Author:	Lisa Yee

In five or fewer sentences, summarize your book so far:

Stanford Wong is struggling in class and has to take summer school so he doesn't flunk English. He also doesn't want his friends to find out about this. So, Millicent Min, a really smart girl, has to tutor him, and she has a best friend who he really likes. But, he doesn't want her to find out that he needs tutoring, and she doesn't want her to know she is smart, so they have to work together to keep their secret. But… he already feels really pressured to do well by his dad, and he doesn't know how to keep all his struggles under control.

Add a photo of part of your conference assignment that shows your best thinking:

aug 26 2021	Stanford Wong flunks Big-Time by Lisa Yee	
Pg # 31	I notice... Stretch comes over to Stanfolds house.	I predict... I predict Stretch isnt going to figure out, but he will get suspicious.
147	Yin-Yin tells Stanford why his dad can be a little hard on him.	I think he will talk to his dad about it

How did your conference assignment help you develop your thinking about *this* text?

It helped me think of his dad's point of view a bit more, and hope they can fix their relationship. Since the book is from Stanford's point of view, you don't really see how his dad feels until his dad talks to him. Then you can see that Stanford didn't see his dad really cared for him a lot even though it didn't feel like it. His dad seemed to like Stanford's sister more.

Describe how this work might help you when you read other books:

Predicting helps me figure out what other characters are thinking or feeling if the author doesn't tell us in the book. It helps me figure out what other characters who aren't the narrator are thinking or feeling instead of just the main character. This will be helpful in lots of other books that have lots of characters.

Sonya Simpson, a teacher at Restoration Academy Middle School in Bedford-Stuyvesant, Brooklyn, devised this tracking sheet.

Jesse Mayer's conference reflection sheet. See page 172 and scholastic.com/RadicalListeningResources for a blank, reproducible version.

Types of Reading Conferences

A conference is by definition responsive teaching. The whole idea is to not go in with a preplanned script, but respond to what we hear from the student. However, that doesn't mean we go in with no idea of possible directions. Sometimes these directions are based on knowledge of a student from formal or informal assessments; sometimes it means picking up from where we left off in the last conference. And yes, it can also mean following up on or extending a whole-class lesson. To confer most effectively with young readers, it's ideal to go in with a plan for where it *might* go— but not be too tied to your plan, in case something better comes up. (Remember, if you don't get to that great teaching point today, there's always the next conference....)

That said, there are types of reading conferences every teacher should know.

A conference is by definition responsive teaching. The whole idea is to not go in with a preplanned script, but respond to what we hear from the student.

The "Getting to Know You" (Assessment) Conference

Most typical toward the beginning of the year or when a student is new to the class, the assessment conference could also happen when we are stumped and not sure where to go next with a student. This sort of conference goes back to the first principle of listening in Chapter One—concentrate on learning before you worry about teaching. It may be helpful to take the opportunity here to be curious, ask questions, jot down interesting things the student says or does, and not stress about coming up with a teaching point. Often, looking over notes after such a conference allows us to come back next time with a clear objective in mind. (Tip: Some teachers find it helpful to keep a copy of the Content-of-Comprehension Cheat Sheet on page 165 in front of them, to listen for evidence of strategies.)

The "Follow Up/Extend a Strategy From Last Time" Conference

It is in the best interest of both teacher and student to feel there is continuity from one conference to the next. Moreover, once we have found the right teaching point for a particular reader it can be extended over several meetings, upping the ante each time. Beginning a new conference by checking in on the teaching point from last time serves a double purpose. First, it sends a message that the strategy from last time is something you can and should carry over to the next book (and the book after that!). Second, it gives the teacher a starting point for the conversation, while still allowing for student ownership. (Sample language: "How is it going deciding which parts to connect in this book?" or "Last time we spoke about paying special attention to facts that surprised you. What surprising facts are you noticing in your new book?")

The "Thinking About Our Thinking" (Metacognitive) Conference

In this type of conference, you:

- listen for evidence of individual comprehension strategies.
- name them in transferable language.
- invite the student to practice and extend them as she continues in her reading.

For example, let's say a young reader makes a prediction about what is going to happen next in her novel by referencing something that happened before (e.g., "I think her dad will forgive her even though she got in trouble, because he was nice the last time she made a mistake."). As teachers, we know this is an

example of making an inference by connecting parts, or synthesizing. We might first name it in kid-friendly language (e.g., "It seems to me you are the kind of reader who thinks backward to think forward. Am I right?"), and then suggest she look for other "think backward to think forward" parts.

The emphasis here is on making students aware of what they do in their heads to understand, so these strategies become conscious tools in their reading tool chest. Once their repertoire is expanded, children become better able to make independent comprehension decisions. After all, to make decisions, you have to know your choices!

The Text-Based Conference

This is a conference focused on "what's on the page" and *not* in a reader's head (e.g., story elements, informational text structures/features, etc.). For example, if a student:

- says, "In this part it's getting exciting," we might respond by teaching about rising action in a story.
- points to illustrations in her nonfiction book, we might teach how to connect regular text with charts or captions.

The "Reinforcing or Extending a Whole-Class Lesson" Conference

Though conferences are about targeting instruction to an individual reader, it's not against the rules to sometimes review or extend a strategy the whole class is working on. This may be an idea from today's lesson, or one from a week or a month ago. A prime objective of conferring is to help children learn to make comprehension decisions independently. With this in mind, it's a good idea to remain on the lookout for instances when students try learned strategies without prompting, and to reinforce that behavior.

Two ways to reinforce or extend a whole-class lesson in a conference are:

- personalize the instruction (e.g., providing additional support, adding a new element).
- encourage reflection. ("How is this strategy helping you understand the book?")

Personalizing the Whole-Class Lesson

If a child is having difficulty understanding or applying a lesson, it can be helpful to use the conference as an opportunity to break it down into smaller chunks and coach her as she practices. For example, third grader Aisha's class in the Bronx was working on nonfiction note-taking. Her book, about cats, had multiple facts on each page—which was clearly overwhelming her. Aisha was jotting down whole sentences verbatim from the book when I approached and asked what she was thinking about so far.

AISHA: I'm thinking there are lots of different kinds of cats. *(Points to an illustration showing different breeds.)*

DAN: There sure are! Is there anything you are learning that you find especially interesting?

AISHA: *(Flips the pages.)* It says here Siamese cats are really friendly and like to cuddle up to their humans.

DAN: Interesting. Why did that fact grab your attention?

AISHA: Because it's not the same for all the other cats.

DAN: Say more about that.

AISHA: *(Points to another illustration.)* It says here the American Shorthair cat doesn't like to be carried.

DAN: Hmm. Aisha, it sounds like this fact reminded you of the other one, about the Siamese cats. Can you tell me about that?

AISHA: Well, they are both about how cats are with people. But they are kind of opposite facts.

DAN: Do you think there may be other ones about cats with people? *(Aisha nods.)* Do you want to start a list of cats-with-people facts in your notebook? *(A. nods again.)* You know, Aisha, what you just did—starting with a fact you thought was interesting, and then finding another one that reminds you of it—could be a good way to take notes, as we've been doing in class.

In this conference, starting with simply asking Aisha what she found interesting—rather than which facts go together—led to her spontaneously grouping the information. Then, naming the category using *her* language (i.e., cats-with-people facts) and connecting it to the class objective of note-taking, put her at ease. From there she was able to come up with several examples of *facts-that-remind-me-of-other-facts*.

> **Teaching Point:** Readers of nonfiction pay special attention to facts that remind them of other facts—and think about how and why they go together.

Encouraging Reflection

When a new comprehension strategy is taught in a reading workshop, teachers usually name it, demonstrate how it works, and give students opportunities to practice. What we often leave out of the equation is asking individual readers to reflect on exactly how the strategy is helping them to understand. As Ellin Keene (2007) reminds us, skilled readers think about their thinking—and a conference is the perfect opportunity to take a 1:1 moment to reflect on how the strategy is working for them personally. This can be done in the form of a simple direct question, e.g., "How is this strategy helping you to understand better?," either as an opener or when it comes up during a conference.

As Ellin Keene (2007) reminds us, skilled readers think about their thinking—and a conference is the perfect opportunity to take a 1:1 moment to reflect on how the strategy is working for them personally.

Second grader Wendy and her classmates at Manhattan's P.S. 41 were transitioning from picture books to chapter books, and recent whole-class lessons had addressed how to keep track of a story when it goes on for many pages with limited picture support. The latest mini-lesson was about readers needing to decide which parts were especially interesting and important. Wendy had chosen a page she wanted to talk about ahead of time from her book, *The Sapphire Princess Meets a Monster*. When I began the conference by checking in on the whole-class work, she ended up getting even more specific about the strategy—and reflecting in a personal way.

DAN: Can you read me the exact part on these pages where you thought "Wow, this is so interesting"?

WENDY: *(Reads aloud)* "That morning a golden basket had very mysteriously arrived at the gates of the Sapphire Palace. A card was pinned to the basket. It read: To the Sapphire Princess. Signed, A Secret Admirer."

DAN: What was interesting about that part for you?

WENDY: I felt like what's gonna happen when she figures out what this golden gift can do, can it give magic powers later in the book?

DAN: So it's sort of a what's-gonna-happen part.

WENDY: Yes. It's really interesting to have a what's-going-to-happen question.

Here, again, is an example of adopting the child's language—by referring to it as a what's-gonna-happen part rather than a prediction, Wendy felt some ownership. This opened an opportunity for reflection.

DAN: It seems to me that you understand one type of part it's really important to pay attention to is a what's-gonna-happen part. Is that true?

WENDY: Yes.

DAN: Tell me about that. Why is it so important to pay attention to the what's-gonna-happen parts?

WENDY: Well, the reason I pay attention to the what's-gonna-happen parts is because I don't know what's gonna happen and I want to find out.

DAN: So it helps you focus on what you want to find out as you keep reading?

WENDY: Yes!

Wendy shares an example from her book in our virtual reading conference.

Asking, "Why is it so important to pay attention to the what's-gonna-happen parts?," I invited Wendy to think about her thinking. As a result, she named for herself how the strategy helped her understand. Picking up on her cue, I got even more specific, suggesting it also helped her focus on what was coming next. Once we'd arrived at this point, she agreed it would be interesting to keep track of what's-gonna-happen parts for the next couple of chapters—and also to note where she found the answers.

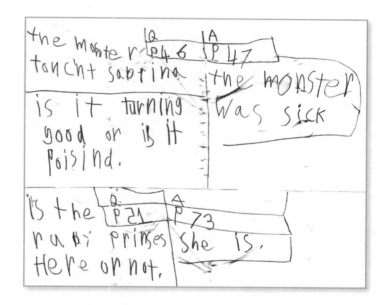

Teaching Point: Readers pay special attention to what's-gonna-happen parts to focus on what's coming next.

Logistical FAQs

It's not just the little things that'll get you. From organizational issues to pedagogical decisions, there are predictable problems that typically come up as we make individual reading conferences part of our comprehension instruction. What follows are not intended as magic bullets, but rather some ideas about how to approach common conundrums.

How do I confer if I haven't read the book?

Assuming we have a well-stocked classroom library or book room, and we're allowing for student choice and voice, the odds are that many—if not most—reading conferences will be about books we haven't read ourselves. As daunting as this seems at first, children and young adult literature is usually pretty predictable in structure. If you've read one book in the Magic Tree House series, chances are you can safely anticipate how another will go. (Morgan LeFay will send Jack and Annie off on an adventure; he will worry, and she will be more reckless.) Most dystopian trilogies for middle school follow a similar pattern as well. (We'll be introduced to a future world with a repressive government, as seen through the eyes of a young protagonist who will set out to change things, usually after encountering a personal challenge.) While it is a good idea for us to read at least one example of a series, author, or genre that's popular with our students, knowing those predictable structures makes it possible to confer into specific titles we haven't read. Do we hear evidence of a student prioritizing certain information in a nonfiction text, or connecting facts across pages? Does that reader of historical fiction seem aware of the significance of the setting, or the way the conflict in the main character's mind relates to the historical period? Listening through the lens of comprehension strategies or qualities of the genre can shine a light on what a child is able to do as a reader, even when we aren't familiar with the specific text.

Listening through the lens of comprehension strategies or qualities of the genre can shine a light on what a child is able to do as a reader, even when we aren't familiar with the specific text.

Ironically, knowing a book too well can sometimes get in the way of listening to the child in front of us. The temptation to perseverate on a missed plot point may interfere with recognizing what a young reader is understanding. As difficult as it may be to let an unnoticed detail go (within reason), odds are a child will not go on to be a worse reader because she missed a nuance or two in the latest Jacqueline Woodson book. And if the student is marveling at a beautiful passage, or coming to a realization about an injustice in the world, or noticing something important about a character, we may inadvertently discourage her thinking by calling attention to every single detail. Again, the priority in a reading conference is to teach the reader, not the book.

What if students choose a book that is too hard?

A third-grade boy comes to school excitedly showing off his Harry Potter book. "I saw the movie over the weekend," he gushes, "so now I want to read the book!" A sixth-grade girl brings Jesmyn Ward's National Book Award winner, *Sing, Unburied, Sing*—a complicated novel with adult themes—to her ELA class. "My older sister said this book was amazing," she explains, "so I really want to try it."

According to Richard Allington and Rachael Gabriel (2012), "reading at 98% or higher accuracy is essential for reading acceleration." At the same time, the research is conclusive on the link between young readers choosing their own books and improved comprehension (Guthrie & Humenick, 2004; Krashen, 2011; and many more!). So what do we do when students pick books that are too hard, or inappropriate for their age?

Is it important for students to spend most of their independent reading time with just-right books? Absolutely. Does this mean they should never be allowed to stray from their designated text level? Not necessarily.

Like most things in education, it's the spirit, not the letter of the law that counts. In other words, while it is essential for a reading teacher to be familiar with the research, she must balance it with her knowledge of the individual child. Is it important for students to spend most of their independent reading time with just-right books? Absolutely. Does this mean they should never be allowed to stray from their designated text level? Not necessarily. Just as adult readers sometimes try out a difficult scientific journal article or a very long and complicated piece of literary fiction (think late Toni Morrison or James Joyce), children should sometimes be allowed to be ambitious and challenge themselves.

At the same time, if a book is so difficult as to be truly out of reach, we run the risk of kids pretending to read and/or becoming disengaged. In such an instance it's our job to gently guide students to more appropriate texts. For example, for that third grade Harry Potter fan, what is an easier magical fantasy series he could read, with Harry as a goal for the future? Maybe the girl with the Jesmyn Ward book is interested in reading about racism in American history, so could try Sharon Draper's *Copper Sun*—for now.

What if a student only ever reads the same type of book?

Most teachers have taught that kid who wants to read only graphic novels. Or Captain Underpants. Or fantasy, or sports, or books about dinosaurs. Of course we want to honor their right to choose, but it is also an educator's job to make sure her students read a variety of genres over the course of a school year. How do we get a child to mix it up and try new things?

First, if we are to be honest, many adult readers don't have a particularly varied reading diet either. (My daughter and I tend to read literary fiction. My partner usually goes for memoirs by women in war-torn countries. My neighbor devours anything about art and photography. And so on.) To the extent that most grown-ups think about their reading personalities at all, it's usually in terms of what type of book they like to read. We may pick up other things when there is a pressing reason, but mostly stick to our preferred sections in the bookstores of the world.

To encourage students to try a variety of texts, we should first honor their preferences. Many a child has been turned off books entirely by being forced to read things they don't want to read. If the objective is for students to vary their choices willingly, it makes sense to begin by allowing them ample time with those darned Wimpy Kid or dinosaur books—and to celebrate those choices. Once students know their preferences are valued, they are often more willing to take a chance with a less familiar genre. My friend and colleague Kathy Collins suggests asking the reader what it is about *this* type of book that makes her want to read it, and guiding her to another title with the same qualities. Then it falls to us (a savvy librarian can be helpful) to recommend other texts that connect in some way to the usual suspects. Does the young reader typically go for graphic novels with monsters? Maybe a fantasy series would be appealing. Is there a student who prefers sad stories with a strong message? Perhaps a Jackie Woodson novel in verse has some of the same qualities. And that kid who is obsessed with dinosaurs may enjoy some science fiction about time travel.

Again, if students feel they have some say in their own reading lives, it's fair to say to them, "My job as your teacher is to be sure you try many kinds of books—but since you are the reader, you get to help decide which things you *want* to try."

CHAPTER FOUR

Individual Writing Conferences

"We write for the same reason that we walk, talk, climb mountains or swim the oceans—because we can. We have some impulse within us that makes us want to explain ourselves to other human beings."

—Maya Angelou

Writing workshop had just ended. The fifth graders in Kristen's class at Midtown West School in New York City were packing up for lunch when I noticed a boy furtively passing a beat-up notebook to his friend at the next table. The front and back covers were covered in colorful cartoon-like doodles of outer-space superheroes, with captions in several different handwritings.

As I approached, the two boys looked up with slightly guilty expressions. The recipient of the notebook, Sharif, stuffed it in his backpack. "What's that?" I asked.

"Oh, nothing," Sharif replied, a bit flustered. "It's not for school."

When writers get to make their own decisions, they feel engaged, produce better work, and just plain try harder.

"It looks interesting," I assured him. "Can I see?" Cautiously, he handed it over.

Inside the frayed notebook was a fantasy story over 30 pages long, every few paragraphs in a different child's handwriting. The quality of the writing was far superior to the persuasive essays Sharif and his friends had been working on in class. The story was filled with sensory details, funny dialogue, and vivid descriptions. Sharif seemed surprised I was interested.

"How do you guys know what happens next in the story with so many people working on it?" I asked.

"We kind of plan it out together," he motioned toward a group of boys, now looking over and smiling. "When you finish your part, you talk to the next person about how it should go, but they get to decide. Sometimes we change stuff if someone comes up with a good idea."

The mismatch was striking. Though the boys produced adequate pieces for writing workshop—dutifully implementing mini-lesson strategies and making their way through a cycle of planning, drafting, revising, and publishing—they didn't compare to the piece in Sharif's notebook. These fifth graders were writing what they wanted to write, making their own revision decisions, and having spontaneous conferences with one another along the way.

Sometimes, of course, students must write things they *don't* get to choose. And clearly it is our job to introduce specific strategies, genres, and structures. But the lesson of Sharif and his fifth-grade fantasy posse is worth considering. When writers get to make their own decisions, they feel engaged, produce better work, and just plain try harder. Moreover, when there is a social component, students benefit from new perspectives and are often more inclined to try new things.

This is where conferring comes in.

No matter the genre we are working on, there is room for student choice. Whether it's a unit on realistic fiction, literary essay, or an all-about book, young writers can decide where to vary sentence lengths, or add a sensory description, or adopt a conversational tone. In a conference, our role is that of facilitator, recognizing what a young writer is trying to do and teaching her useful writing strategies to accomplish that goal. Conferences can and should be opportunities to help children become independent writing decision-makers.

It's important to remember that teaching into student decision-making is not just an incidental part of writing instruction. In fact, the act of writing is intrinsically *about* deciding what you want to say and choosing the words that will best express it. Scardamalia and Bereiter (1987) point out the difference between a *knowledge telling* approach to writing, where young writers record their ideas without reflection, to a more mature *knowledge transforming* approach, where they make decisions to clarify and extend their thinking. In other words, as a mature writer tries to figure out which words to put on the page, she goes back and forth between thinking about what she wants to say and figuring out *how* to say it—and as a result, her ideas develop and grow. As Flannery O'Connor put it, "I write because I don't know what I think until I read what I say."

> "Most of the basic material a writer works with is acquired before the age of fifteen."
> —WILLA CATHER

Before delving into the particulars of what goes into a good writing conference, I would be remiss to not acknowledge the wisdom and insights of my co-conspirator and buddy Carl Anderson. He will be appropriately credited along the way, but pretty much all my thinking on the subject is directly or indirectly related to lessons I've learned from him.

Breaking It Down: What Is an Individual Writing Conference?

When my daughter Sonia was three years old, she had a keen eye for what other people were doing. In my off hours from teaching, I was working as a musician, and much to her chagrin spent hours composing at an electronic piano. She would stand at the door impatiently, watching me scribble notes on music paper.

One day, after a short break, I returned to the study to find her wearing my adult-sized headphones, banging the piano keys, stopping now and then to draw large, colorful dots on the manuscript paper with a colored marker.

"What are you doing?" I asked.

Sonia looked up, a businesslike expression on her face. "I'm being a man."

In their efforts to understand the world, children are keenly aware of and naturally curious about the roles played by those around them. At the same time, they are developmentally wired to see things through the lens of their own experience. A young child writing about her mom sees no need to describe what she looks or acts like because, after all, how could anyone *not* know her mom?

On one hand, teaching a student to make decisions as she writes is teaching her to think more deeply. That's the internal part, figuring out exactly what we are trying to say. But there's also the external part, putting ourselves in the mind of a reader to effectively communicate an idea, feeling, or question. "Try to read your own work as a stranger would read it," quips Zadie Smith, "or even better, as an enemy would."

Imagining how someone else will experience their writing does not come naturally to most children. This, too, comes down to decision-making—what strategy should I use to make the reader feel as I feel, understand as I understand? Our job in a writing conference is to bridge that gap—to teach a student to "hold in mind both his or her writerly intentions and the imagined response of the reader to the emerging text" (Myhill, Lines, & Jones, 2020). In other words, to see a piece of writing through the eyes of the reader. What information do I need to include that she or he might not know? What words will evoke a feeling or reaction? How can I phrase my message in such a way that my reader will be curious and remain interested? (Apart from helping them become better writers, developing this sort of literary empathy can also have a welcome ripple effect on how students communicate in the world outside of school!)

As with a reading conference, to confer effectively with a young writer requires a diagnostic ear, an understanding of basic conference structure, and content knowledge. Though the basic competencies are the same, there is, of course, different content we teach in a writing conference.

> "On paper, things can live forever. On paper, a butterfly never dies."
> —JACQUELINE WOODSON

The Qualities of Writing: What We Teach When We Teach Writing

Narrowing down which qualities of writing to teach can be confusing. Depending on where you look, they are defined in multiple ways—and different things are prioritized. An Internet search for "Qualities of Writing" turns up a wide array of possibilities.

According to Ruth Culham in her popular book *6+1 Traits of Writing* (2003), it boils down to:

- ideas
- organization
- voice
- word choice
- sentence fluency
- conventions
- presentation

In his touchstone book *A Teacher's Guide to Writing Conferences* (2019), Carl Anderson defines the qualities of writing as follows:

- focus
- structure
- detail
- voice
- conventions

Lucy Calkins and her colleagues at the Teachers College Reading and Writing Project, in their *Writing Pathways* (2014) assessment continuum, break the qualities into three categories, each with subheadings:

Structure

- overall
- lead
- transitions
- ending
- organization

Development

- elaboration
- craft

Language Conventions

- spelling
- punctuation

The Common Core State Anchor Standards for Writing prioritize the "Production and Distribution of Writing," and call on students to:

- Produce clear and coherent writing in which the *development*, *organization*, and *style* are appropriate to task, purpose, and audience.
- Develop and strengthen writing as needed by *planning*, *revising*, *editing*, *rewriting*, or trying a new approach.

It's enough to make you dizzy. Whom to believe? Fortunately, a closer look at these names and definitions reveal they are, in fact, not so different. Structure is essentially organization; focus and detail have everything to do with elaboration; voice aligns with craft and style, etc.

Most writing conferences fall into four general categories:

- **Structure/Organization:** This could refer to the macro (e.g., the way an entire piece is organized from beginning to end) or to the micro (e.g., the way a paragraph, sentence, or sequence of sentences are put together).
- **Focus/Detail/Elaboration:** Where to say more, where to say less; what to emphasize and what not to emphasize; which details to include—or not (e.g., a visual description, a fact or statistic, etc.).
- **Craft/Voice:** This one is the most difficult to explain, and often overlaps with other qualities. It has to do with the artistic, individual aspects of writing. Examples could include tone (e.g., formal vs. informal, conversational, etc.);

use of literary devices (e.g., alliteration, onomatopoeia); the specific way an author describes characters, actions, and settings, etc. Voice and craft may differ depending on the audience we are writing for as well.

- **Conventions:** Anything to do with the nuts and bolts of writing, such as punctuation, grammar, capitalization, or spelling. The term is often used to refer to how these things are traditionally used in particular types of writing. It's important to remember, though, that the "rules" differ depending on the genre. For example, it would be bad form to start a sentence with "And" in a business letter or scientific article, but it is often done in a newspaper editorial or piece of fiction.

> "I try to leave out the parts that people skip."
> —ELMORE LEONARD

Though writing units are often focused on genre, it is a mistake to let genre dictate the qualities of writing we teach in a conference. Any fourth grader having difficulty with structure in a personal narrative is likely to *also* have issues with structure in an opinion essay; and a seventh grader skilled at elaboration in her feature article is likely to be good at it in her realistic fiction piece as well. One of the secrets to conferring effectively with young writers is thinking of teaching points related to qualities of writing, rather than characteristics of a specific genre.

Certain teaching points may bridge more than one quality. For example, varying sentence lengths impacts not only a paragraph's structure, but also its voice. It is a good idea to spend time at the start of the school year deciding on which qualities of writing to focus on with individual students, and stick with them for several conferences—even if the class has moved on to a new genre of writing. (Tip: If you notice similar patterns across your class, it's not cheating to repeat similar teaching points with more than one student!)

Carl Anderson points out that another factor that may determine the direction of a writing conference is the stage of the *writing cycle* (2019). In other words, the appropriate teaching point sometimes depends on where a student is in the process of developing her piece.

As with the qualities of writing, depending on which resource you consult, the stages of this cycle are defined somewhat differently. According to MIT's 2020 Resources for Writers, "Writing is a process that involves at least four distinct steps: prewriting, drafting, revising, and editing/proofreading." Most sources include some version of those steps, which may be defined on page 94.

- **Prewriting:** What a writer typically does to prepare. This includes all aspects of planning, e.g., thinking ahead about how to structure the piece, what content to put in, etc. It could also refer to coming up with a worthwhile topic or thesis.
- **Drafting:** The first (or second, or third) attempt at writing a complete piece.
- **Revising:** After drafting, reading the piece over and changing specific parts for the better. To see again: *re-vise*.
- **Editing/Proofreading:** Once the piece is mostly done, fixing any small mistakes (e.g., spelling errors, typos, missing punctuation, etc.) you may have overlooked.

Writers often follow these steps in order—but not always. A conversation with a dozen writers about how they go about creating a piece will likely reveal a dozen different approaches. When I interviewed the wonderful memoirist Frank McCourt, author of *Angela's Ashes* and *'Tis*, he told me he liked to "bash out the whole thing in longhand on yellow legal pads, no stopping" and then revise when he retyped the draft onto his computer. Other writers (myself included) tend to revise as they go, looking back at earlier sections and changing them every time they sit down to write. As Kurt Vonnegut memorably put it, "Swoopers write a story quickly, higgledy-piggledy, crinkum-crankum, any which way. Then they go over it again painstakingly, fixing everything that is just plain awful or doesn't work. Bashers go one sentence at a time, getting it exactly right before they go on to the next one. When they're done, they're done."

> "People almost never change without first feeling understood."
> —DOUGLAS STONE

Though we don't want to insist students write in a lockstep sequence, we do want them to be aware of the thinking work involved in each step. Again, from MIT: "(Writing) is known as a recursive process. While you are revising, you might have to return to the prewriting step to develop and expand your ideas." There is no wrong or right way to write, but writers typically consider different things depending where they are on the road to a finished piece. To come up with appropriate teaching points, teachers should be aware of where students are in the writing cycle.

To illustrate the idea of listening with these factors in mind, the chart on the next page lays out a few (far from all!) examples of teaching points for each category.

QUALITIES OF WRITING/WRITING CYCLE: A CHEAT SHEET FOR CONFERRING

QUALITIES OF WRITING
What we teach when we teach writing, regardless of genre

Structure/Organization
MACRO:
- Transitions, i.e., how to get from one section of a piece to the next
- Reordering sections of a piece
- Story structure, e.g., where and how to introduce characters, problem, solution, etc.
- Essay structure, e.g., thesis statement, examples, conclusion
- Informational text structure, e.g., topic sentence, sequence and grouping of information
- Informational text features, e.g., captions, subtitles, graphs, and charts

MICRO:
- Thinking about the sequence of sentences in a specific paragraph, e.g., varying sentence length, putting information in an appropriate order, etc.

Focus/Detail/Elaboration
- Which parts need additional sensory or descriptive detail
- Which parts require additional info or explanation
- Where to take out unnecessary detail
- Deciding which sections should be longer or shorter

Craft/Voice
- "Talking to the reader," i.e., writing in a conversational tone
- Combining action and description in the same sentence (e.g., "Her black dreadlocks bounced up and down as she ran toward the goal line")
- Following a long, multi-clause sentence with a very short one, for emphasis
- Showing (not telling) character emotion through facial expression and/or movement
- Conveying a mood through setting description
- Describing by comparing (e.g., metaphor/simile/ personification)
- Varying the signifying verb in dialogue, e.g., "she exclaimed" vs. "she said"

Conventions
- Dividing a sentence into clauses
- Varying ending punctuation
- Punctuating dialogue
- Following a long clause with a short one
- Using punctuation to create pauses

STAGES OF THE WRITING CYCLE
What we may teach at different points in the writing process

Prewriting
- Planning out the sections of a piece with a graphic organizer (e.g., flow chart, timeline, outline)
- Narrowing down a topic with a semantic web
- Freewrite about your topic to generate content
- Gather information about a nonfiction topic

Drafting
- Engaging lede
- Rising action (narrative)
- Reflective conclusion (essay, narrative)
- Varying internal thinking/feeling and external action (narrative)
- Expository text structures (e.g., question/ answer, cause/effect, problem/solution, chronological)
- Summative conclusion (expository)

Revising
- Almost anything in drafting can also be taught during revision
- Reordering sections in a larger piece, or sentences in a specific section
- Word choice: using more unique or descriptive vocabulary
- Where to add dialogue, or sensory detail, or physical description
- Taking out parts that seem redundant or too long
- Mixing up long and short sentences, to keep it interesting

Editing/Proofreading
- Checking for typos, spelling, punctuation, syntax, grammar mistakes
- Checking for unnecessary repetition
- Looking for places where sentences that are too long may be broken up into shorter ones
- Looking for places where shorter sentences may be combined into longer, more complex ones

Go to page 167 and scholastic.com/RadicalListeningResources for a reproducible/downloadable version of this sheet.

Structure of a Writing Conference: A Step-Wise Approach

One thing that may make a writing conference feel easier than a reading conference from a teacher's perspective is having something concrete to look at. But from the student's point of view, that can be scary. Many adults feel vulnerable when they show someone else their writing, and children are no different.

> "It's easy enough to tell what is wrong. But that's not what I want to hear all night long."
> —LOU REED

Who can blame them? As a profession, we teachers tend to accentuate the negative. Most of us look at a piece of student writing and immediately notice what the child *can't* do. The resulting one-on-one conversation ends up being a verbal equivalent of red penning the work. So today's piece ends up improved, but has the student learned something that will make her a better writer moving forward?

Even the most fledgling writer has something she does best. Yes, a conference should begin with a compliment, but if it quickly moves to what is wrong with the piece, children learn over time that the real reason you are here is to tell them what they *can't* do.

Ideally, the teaching point in a writing conference should extend the most sophisticated thing that student is beginning to understand—again, the zone of proximal development. Often that partial understanding can be a bridge to addressing a need (e.g., "You are doing a great job including dialogue in your story. Let me teach you how authors sometimes go inside their characters' heads to tell what those characters are *thinking*"), but generally speaking, a conference is not a remedial session. One way of thinking about this is if every time you and I have a conversation, the subject is what you do least well, you are *not* going to look forward to my visits. Our hope is that a student will look forward to each conference, and expect her teacher to recognize something she can do that maybe she didn't even know she *could* do—and have confidence in her ability to go further.

The key to teaching a student something about writing that she can internalize and then use in future pieces of writing is in *how* we say it. Though the structure of a writing conference is similar to a reading conference, there are some important differences. My buddy Carl Anderson (again!) and I have compared notes, and together came up with this step-wise approach.

Steps in a Writing Conference

RESEARCH AND DISCOVER

1 **Start with a thinking question,** e.g., "What are you working on in today's writing?" If the student has difficulty explaining, ask what part she is working on.

2 **Scan the writing quickly to get an idea of the kind of work the student is doing.**

3 **Ask the student to describe or show a specific part** in her writing that shows what she is working on.

4 **Ask her to say more about that thing.** Ask more than once.

ASSESS AND DECIDE

5 **Look and listen for a partial understanding.** Which quality of writing can you build on?

6 **Prioritize a direction for teaching.** Use the student's partial understanding as a jumping-off point for teaching something new about writing (ZPD).

TEACH

7 **State a teaching point** that extends the partial understanding, in language that can apply to the next piece of writing, and the piece of writing after that. (Show an example in a mentor text, when possible.)

8 **Have the student apply the teaching point** to today's piece of writing (a "try it"). Negotiate parameters with the student, such as how many examples, where in the piece to try it, etc.

9 **Articulate the teaching point** as a final comment, connecting it to future writing, e.g., "Doing this work will help you practice…"

Go to page 168 and scholastic.com/RadicalListeningResources for a reproducible/downloadable version of these steps.

Conference With Carrie

To see these steps in action, let's look at an actual writing conference.

Carrie is a fourth grader in Shenzhen, China, participating in the Ming Yang Writing Mastery Program. Though her first language is Mandarin, instruction at her school is largely in English. A shy girl with a quiet voice, Carrie showed a keen awareness of literary elements but seemed a bit uncomfortable explaining her thinking. She was working on a personal narrative about a family trip to the northern part of Vietnam in winter, her first experience with snow.

DAN: Hi, Carrie! What are you working on right now in your writing? **1**

CARRIE: I'm writing some descriptions of how it looked on my vacation. About the setting.

DAN: Wow! You have some vivid descriptions here. *(Dan scans the writing.)* I notice you used a lot of commas. Can you tell me about that? **2**

CARRIE: It's so you can take a breath when you read it.

DAN: I see. It works really well! What made you decide to put breaths in those exact places?

after wearing all these things, we got out side. The mountain is enourmous ~~aff~~ and high, covered with snow, it's glorious. We started climbing the mountain. The wind blows the trees right and left, foward and backwards. There's snow everywhere, covering the

CARRIE: *(Pauses, thinks)* I don't know.

DAN: Would it help to read it out loud?

CARRIE: Maybe.

DAN: Let's try it.

CARRIE: Okay. *(Reads)* "The mountain is enormous and high, covered
            with snow, it's glorious. We started climbing the mountain.
            The wind blows the trees right and left, forward and backward."

DAN: So what do you think?

CARRIE: The commas make you stop and get ready for the next part.
            So they sort of connect. ❸

❷ I begin the conference by asking what Carrie is working on *as a writer*, rather
than what the piece is about. This sets the stage for a conversation about the
qualities of writing rather than the plot of her story. It also sends a message that
we are two writers having a conversation, and I am interested in what you are
thinking about.

❷ ❸ Here, I quickly look over the writing for something Carrie has done that hints
at a *partial understanding*—and ask her to reflect on it. Often this is something the
child hasn't done consciously, and she may feel caught off guard. It is important
to not come to the student's rescue too quickly and answer for her. Given a little
time, most young writers will rise to the occasion. In this instance, asking Carrie
to read a specific section out loud provided a concrete strategy *for* thinking about
what she was doing as a writer.

DAN: Interesting. I notice that some of the parts are longer than
            others. *(Points)* Like here, the first part has six words—"The
            mountain is enormous and high"—the next part has three,
            "covered with snow"—and then the last one has only two—
            "it's glorious." Can you tell me about that? ❹

CARRIE: Well, the first told what it was about, the mountain—so that
            had to be long. Then the next part told what it looked like,
            and the last part told how it felt.

DAN: So you saved the feeling part until last. Say more about that. **④**

CARRIE: *(Thinks for a moment)* I guess after I told how the mountain looked, it was important to tell how it felt. And it was better to make it short, after the long parts.

DAN: So you saved the important bit for last, *and* you made it short. This is a really interesting writing strategy. You showed a thing is important by making it short—and then you put that short part right after some longer parts, so it really stands out to the reader. Would you like to learn how to go even further with that? **⑤**

CARRIE: *(Smiles)* Okay.

④ Quoting the student's writing is a powerful move that signals *her* words are important. Resist the temptation to paraphrase! And then, of course, ask the child to say more about that.

⑤ Naming what the student did in transferable language, which can apply to other pieces of writing than the one in front of you, is *the* critical move in a conference. Here I name it and invite Carrie to go further. This lets her know the teaching point is coming—and that it came from what *she* did.

DAN: One thing authors can do to make their writing more interesting is use sentences of different lengths—some long and some short. *(Takes out a copy of* Because of Winn-Dixie, *the class read-aloud)* Check out how Kate DiCamillo does it. *(Reads aloud)* "And then the dog came running around the corner. He was a big dog. And ugly." Just like you did with the commas, she goes from long to medium to short—only with sentences. And that last one, "And ugly," really stands out. **⑥** Is there a place in your story where you can try mixing up some short and long sentences? **⑦**

CARRIE: *(Scans her work)* Maybe in this part, where my dad starts swinging my sister around. I could tell about him swinging her in a long sentence and then tell how she felt in a short one.

DAN: Fabulous. I'll come back in a few minutes to check in. **8**

6 Here is the teaching point, an extension of Carrie's partial understanding. When possible, demonstrating with a familiar mentor text (*Because of Winn-Dixie* was the class read-aloud) makes the lesson more concrete.

7 Having the student "try it" right away allows her to take ownership.

8 Carl Anderson recommends having students try out the new teaching point strategy immediately, then returning to wrap up the conference. I left Carrie at this point to work on her own, without the looming presence of an expectant adult hovering over her shoulder. Leaving for a few minutes served the double purpose of allowing her to independently try using the new strategy, as well as giving me the opportunity to start conferring with another student. Once *that* writer had a teaching point to try out, I returned to Carrie.

DAN: So how'd it go?

CARRIE: Good. Can I show you what I wrote?

My dad swung my sister, like riding a rollercoaster, her cheeks are red as tomato, then my dad swung her in a nother poshiton, it's like swinging a swing. My sister's heart pounded with excitement.

DAN: So interesting how you used all the commas in the long sentence and then followed it with that short sentence about how your sister felt. From now on, whenever you write, you can think about mixing up short and long sentences—and use short ones to get the reader's attention. **9** What do you think?

CARRIE: I think it will really help my writing.

DAN: Great. I'm excited to see how that works for you in your
            writing from now on! **9**

9 It is important to end the conference by coming back to the teaching point, stated in language that can apply to the next piece of writing, and the piece after that. And then set the expectation that the student will incorporate the lesson into her future writing.

For this conference, I followed the steps in order with little variation. Though Carrie was a girl of few words, grounding the conference in the concrete—e.g., asking her to read specific parts out loud, quoting her precise words rather than paraphrasing, connecting the teaching point to a partial understanding, and having her try out the strategy immediately—allowed for a feeling of ownership. Carrie left the conversation feeling like she played an integral part in determining the lesson.

Diagnostic Listening: What Did Carrie Teach Us?

Carrie's conference was an example of a familiar scenario. Though her piece showed some understanding of literary elements, she was unaccustomed to explaining her writing decisions—if in fact they were decisions at all. It's possible, even likely, that Carrie wasn't intentionally using different-length clauses in a sentence and ending with a short one for emphasis.

Just like learning to talk, children pick up language from books, which they begin to imitate in their writing without even knowing it. By catching them in the act and shining a light on such moments, a teacher can not only help this literary language become a conscious tool in their writing repertoire—something they can use intentionally in the future—but also push them to go further.

The teaching in a writing conference can be seen as a three-step process:

- First, through questioning the student and scanning today's work, we decide on a quality of writing to focus on, based on her partial understanding. This could be suggested by the current piece, or a goal we've identified for that student over time. (*Will today's conference be about elaboration or structure? At our last meeting we focused on conventions, so should we continue with that today?*)
- Next, we name and compliment the student's partial understanding, using transferable language she can apply to future writing as well.
- Finally, we up the ante and extend the teaching point, inviting the student to go even further. This naming acts as a vote of confidence, and the young writer is usually willing to give the teaching point a try.

Though Carrie clearly knew something about how to describe a setting and was beginning to understand the potential of commas, I suspect paying attention to the length of clauses had never occurred to her before this conference. By hearing story language in her reading, she had internalized the technique of using a short phrase for emphasis, but until I pointed it out hadn't realized it. Trying the technique right away allowed me to assess whether the lesson had sunk in. Just as important, it helped Carrie solidify and internalize her new learning.

Teaching Point: Writers use a mix of long and short sentences to make their pieces more interesting. A short sentence (or clause) coming right after a long one can show something is important.

Writing Conferences in Action: A Few More Examples Addressing Various Qualities of Writing

What Do We Look for When We Scan Student Work?

Most students are rarely asked to reflect on their writing decisions. Moreover, they learn quickly if they wait long enough we will probably fill in the blank and do the heavy lifting for them. Asking young writers to reflect on their thinking in a nonjudgmental way signals confidence in their ability to explain—and an interest in what they have to say. This creates a safe space for them to take a chance, and over time they usually rise to the occasion.

Asking young writers to reflect on their thinking in a nonjudgmental way signals confidence in their ability to explain—and an interest in what they have to say.

It takes practice for children to clearly articulate what they are working on as writers; this is one of the most important functions of a conference. At first it feels intimidating, and they lack the language and the lens to discuss their writing strategies. One way to scaffold and help students develop this muscle is to scan their work for the most interesting thing they did in their piece—intentionally or not—and ask them to talk about it.

Many of us feel something similar to the child's intimidation when looking at student work in this way. Thankfully, although every learner is unique in her or his own way, once a teacher has been working with a specific second- or fourth- or seventh-grade class for a length of time, certain patterns begin to emerge. And just as the children get better at discussing their writing with repeated practice, adults feel more comfortable analyzing what they are doing as writers the more they do it.

What follows are excerpts from elementary conferences focusing on specific qualities of writing, at different stages of the writing cycle. In each conference, scanning the work and listening to what the student had to say led to a teaching point useful not just for the current piece, but future writing as well. At the end of each example is the generalizable teaching point, as stated to the student at the end of the conference.

Angelina, Third Grade: Combining Action With Description and Dialogue (elaboration conference)

Angelina is a third grader at a bilingual school in Shenzhen, China. Her personal narrative below, about starting swimming lessons, showed a good grasp of how to write dialogue, as well as a bit of inner thinking ("I wanted to hide. I wanted to run."). Scanning her work, I was impressed with the way Angelina used show-not-tell to describe her feelings ("But my legs are not moving an inch."). She seemed on the verge of understanding how to combine different writing strategies to create a picture in the reader's mind—an elaboration technique.

> I wanted to hide. I wanted to run. But my legs are not moving an inch. "Do I really need to learn this?" I asked my mom. "Learn before you have any comments." my mom replied. "Just learn."

DAN: I notice you described how your body looked in the part about your legs shaking, and you put it right after the wanting to hide and wanting to run sentences. Can you tell me about that?

ANGELINA: Well, I was trying to show that I was scared and didn't want to do it.

DAN: But you never said you were scared.

ANGELINA: Yes, but my body showed it. That's called when you show-not-tell. We learned that in school.

DAN: Interesting. Can you tell me more about that?

ANGELINA: *(Pauses, thinks)* When I put together describing my legs with wanting to run, it showed what I was feeling. Also I put in what we were saying so you could imagine it.

DAN: Angelina, you are on to something very important. Writers often combine things in their stories, just like you put together a thinking part, a description part, and some dialogue. I'd like to teach you how to add one other thing in the mix so a reader can really imagine your feelings.

ANGELINA: Okay. That would be cool.

DAN: Sometimes authors show how a character feels by telling what they are doing. In other words, they show feeling through action—and sometimes they combine it with other things, like dialogue or description. Let's try it. What were you doing in this scene?

ANGELINA: I was shouting. And my body was shaking. Especially my legs.

DAN: Do you think adding that information would help the reader understand how you were feeling? *(Angelina nods.)* I'm going to leave you for a few minutes to try it. Once you finish, see if you can find another place to add another action as well.

> My palms are sweaty and my legs are shaking. "I don't know it! I just don't know it!" I shouted as mom pushed me out of the door. "I don't know how to swim!" "So you have to learn," said my mom. "Or else, you'll never know it."

When I returned, Angelina proudly showed me the revised opening to her story above. Not only had she added her own actions, but also those of her mom. "She was so angry she started pushing me out the door!" Angelina explained. "So I put that in with the dialogue."

Angelina's partial understanding was the idea that you can use more than one writing strategy at the same time (i.e., *thinking, description, dialogue*) to help the reader imagine a feeling. Once I'd *helped her internalize this idea by asking about it ("...together* they showed what I was feeling"), I invited her to go further by adding action to the mix.

Teaching Point: One way writers can show character feelings is by putting action together with descriptions and dialogue.

Imani, Second Grade: Talking to the Reader by Using a Conversational Tone (craft/voice conference)

As very young writers begin to compose longer texts with more words on a page, establishing an engaging tone becomes a challenge. Some sentences are bare bones, with little attention paid to interesting word choice; others run on too long with no discernible end in sight. This is particularly evident in early attempts at information writing, where in their efforts to include facts children often forget about craft. The idea that an author is supposed to keep a reader interested is in fact a relatively new one. "Writers connect with readers by using a consistent tone," asserts Stacy Shubitz (2016). "One way they do this is by adopting a conversational voice."

Imani, a second grader in Harlem, New York, was working on a procedural, "how-to" piece when I sat down to chat with her. (See her piece on pages 108–110.)

DAN: Hi, Imani! You look very busy. What are you working on?

IMANI: Well, I just learned how to tie my shoe *(proudly points to her shoe)*, so now I'm gonna teach it to other kids.

DAN: That sounds very useful. Tell me about how you are teaching them.

IMANI: I'm telling all the steps. Like first you make a loop and then bunny ears. Do you want me to show you?

DAN: Thanks. I'm interested in how you are going to write it. Can you say more about the steps?

IMANI: Well, I'm giving the steps so kids can know what to do.

DAN: It sounds like you are really thinking about your audience, the kids who are going to be reading your piece.

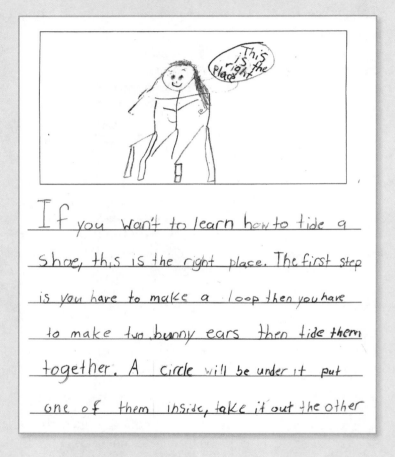

IMANI: Well, I'm a kid, too, and I just learned, so I know what they need to know. And I'm telling them.

DAN: So you are imagining who will be reading your piece, and talking to them. Am I right?

IMANI: Yes.

DAN: I'm wondering about something. In the first sentence you wrote, "If you want to learn to tie a shoe, this is the right place." That part sounded like your voice talking, and it got me interested. Can you tell me about that?

IMANI: Well, it wasn't one of the steps, but I wanted to tell what it was about so they would be ready. And I just told them like I was talking.

From her comments it was clear Imani was putting herself in the reader's place ("...I know what they need to know. And I'm telling them..."), and scanning her work, I noticed a beginning understanding of

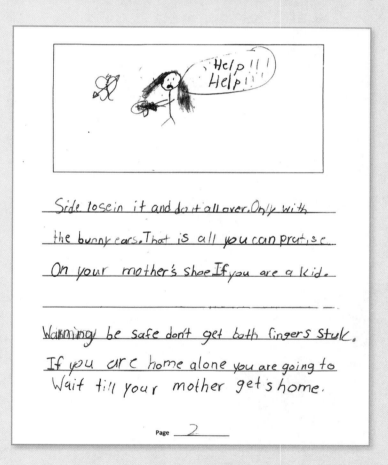

When you do this be careful with it, hope you have a great time, make sure you don't make a not a little not is fine. A big one is not fine be carful you have to do it before your moter goes to work.

Page 3

conversational tone ("If you want to learn to tie a shoe, this is the right place."). Her instructions were clear and to the point, but dry in tone. Put together, she seemed ready for a lesson in balancing this clarity with talking to the reader. And so, the teaching point.

DAN: One way writers can keep their readers interested is mixing talking parts with information parts, just like you did in that sentence. Do you think it would make it interesting to mix in more talking-to-the-reader parts?

IMANI: Yes. I could tell them to be careful and give advice. Like you not getting your fingers stuck.

Imani continued enthusiastically drafting and went on to dispense other valuable advice (e.g.,"You can practice on your mother's shoe if you are a kid.") Her piece shifted to a conversational tone, still spelling out the necessary steps. (See her piece on pages 108–110.) Predictably, once Imani shared her new strategy with the class, many of her fellow second graders began "talking to the reader" routinely in their information pieces.

Teaching Point: Information writers can make their pieces interesting by writing as though they are talking to the reader.

Min, Fourth Grade: Balancing Internal Thinking and External Action (structure/elaboration conference)

When upper-elementary students begin to write longer, multi-page narratives, they often include every single detail—what Lucy Calkins (1994) calls "bed-to-bed" stories, which start when they wake up and end when they go to sleep. Once they've learned to prioritize certain events over others, a typical next stage is recounting one important event after another—with little or no internal thinking.

Min, a fourth grader from Shenzhen, China, fit this pattern. The draft of his "small moment" piece about feeding a kangaroo on page 112 showed some awareness of elaboration (e.g., "...my little hands full of tiny yummy biscuits"), but lacked reflection. Our conference felt like a good opportunity to extend his partial understanding of descriptive, external detail to inner thinking and feeling—and consider how to balance what was in his head with "what happened."

DAN: Hi, Min! What are you working on today as a writer?

MIN: I'm telling about the moment I fed a kangaroo. It was shocking.

DAN: Wow. Shocking, eh? Say more about that.

MIN: When I first saw the kangaroo, it was so big I felt scared to feed it. Especially to put my hand near its mouth. I thought it might bite me. But then I got some courage.

DAN: Can you tell me more about the scared feeling you had when you saw the kangaroo?

MIN: I was worried, and my heart was pounding.

DAN: What an interesting detail, about your heart. I am noticing in your story so far you have other small details—for example, you said "little hands full of tiny yummy biscuits." Tell me about that.

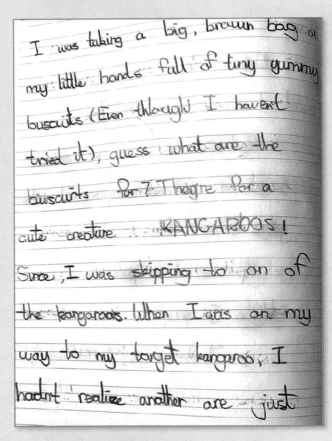

I was taking a big, brown bag or my little hands full of tiny yummy buscuits (Even though I haven't tried it), guess what are the buscuits for? They're for a cute creature... KANGAROOS! Since, I was skipping to on of the kangaroos. When I was on my way to my target kangaroo, I hadn't realize another are just

MIN: When you put in little details, it helps make a movie in your mind.

Scanning his work, it was evident Min had some understanding of the effectiveness of including carefully chosen details (e.g., *little hands*, *tiny yummy biscuits*) to make a story more interesting. What he hadn't yet done was apply this notion to internal feelings or thoughts. Leveraging his strength (small details) to move to the next level (internal feelings) seemed like the way to go.

DAN: I'd like to teach you another way to use details, to show what characters feel inside.

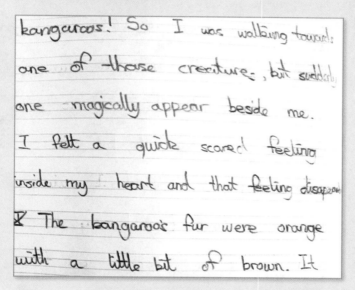

kangaroos! So I was walking towards one of those creatures, but suddenly one magically appear beside me. I felt a quick scared feeling inside my heart and that feeling disappear. The kangaroo's fur were orange with a little bit of brown. It

MIN: Okay.

DAN: Let me show you an example. Do you remember the part in Ralph Fletcher's story "The Last Kiss" when his father stopped shaking his hand? He puts in some details about what he did, but also about how he felt. Listen to the way Ralph writes it: "To my great surprise, he reached out and shook my hand. At first I just felt confused." He tells what the character did— he shook his hand—but also that he felt confused. One way authors can use detail is to mix up action—what the character did—with how they felt inside.

MIN: So maybe I could add the detail about my heart pounding?

DAN: Do you think it would make the story more interesting?

MIN: I think so. And maybe I could find other details about what I was feeling inside.

Pleased with his new discovery, Min promptly added the line "I felt a quick scared feeling inside my heart and that feeling disappeared." (See his piece below.) When I checked back a few minutes later and suggested balancing feelings and action in future writing, he eagerly agreed.

Here's an excerpt from the completed draft he turned in the next day, complete with drumroll:

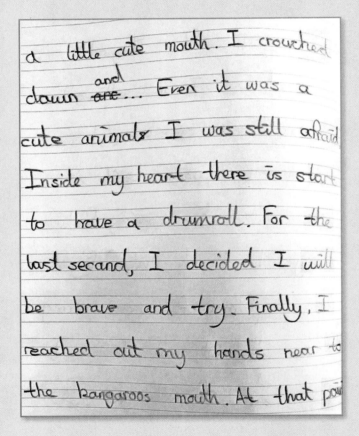

> a little cute mouth. I crouched down and one... Even it was a cute animals I was still afraid Inside my heart there is start to have a drumroll. For the last second, I decided I will be brave and try. Finally, I reached out my hands near to the kangaroos mouth. At that poi

---

Teaching Point: Writers can balance details about what happens on the outside with what characters are feeling or thinking inside.

What Do We Listen for When There Is No Work to Look at?

As tricky as it is to come up with a teaching point by quickly scanning student work, it can be even trickier to do so without something concrete to look at. Whether a young writer is just coming up with a topic or beginning to plan out a new piece, there are times in the writing process when there is no visible evidence of a student's understanding. Conferring in these moments can be especially complicated. Certainly, each child has ongoing goals for us to fall back on, based on prior work and past conferences, which are important to keep in mind whether or not there is work to look at. But if the objective is to be responsive in the moment and allow for ownership and voice, we must draw out students, listen to them, and help them realize their intentions. To do this effectively means drawing on content knowledge of the qualities of writing, with the aim of identifying a strategy that addresses what a child wants to communicate.

The following two middle school conferences occurred at stages in the writing process where the writer had not yet produced any work to guide the way. Consequently, the first part of the conference was devoted more than usual to the specifics of what the writer wanted to say, and its desired effect on the reader.

Makani and Iris, Seventh Grade: Comma Decisions (two-conventions conference)

The teaching of conventions in general, and punctuation in particular, is often approached as a set of rules to be memorized and followed. As I argue in *Practical Punctuation* (2008), authors make choices about how to use punctuation to convey voice, provide emphasis, and establish a mood, among other craft moves. Though there are conventional ways to use grammar and punctuation in particular types of writing, there are few hard and fast rules that hold true across all genres. Common comma usage in a business letter would be out of place in a novel or poem, to cite one of many examples.

Quite apart from dispelling the myth that there are iron-clad, correct ways to use conventions, when students learn that punctuation is something they can make choices about, they tend to think about it more. As a result, they become thoughtful punctuation decision-makers rather than obedient punctuation rule followers.

Back to commas. As essayist Pico Iyer reflected in a 2014 interview for the *Times of India*, "Every day, at my desk, I spend most of my time taking out commas, or putting them in again to catch a certain rhythm, a tone of voice, a slant of light." Iyer is not alone. Many writers consider the "humble comma" (Pico again) more a craft tool than something strictly rule-bound. This particular punctuation mark presents myriad possibilities for an upper-elementary or middle school writer looking to explore more complex sentences and shades of meaning.

Makani, a seventh grader at Taipei American School, was just starting to draft a personal narrative about getting hit by a garbage truck while riding his bike. His class had recently finished reading Sandra Cisneros's short story "Eleven."

> DAN: So what are you working on as a writer?
>
> MAKANI: I'm trying to describe the moment when I got hit. It was weird. I was really scared, but at the same time I was upset about my bike getting ruined.
>
> DAN: Sounds like you were experiencing two different emotions at once.
>
> MAKANI: Yeah, exactly. But at the same time, which made it weird. Like I was worried but also angry.

DAN:	Can you tell me more about that?
MAKANI:	Well, I started out just being shocked, but then my feelings kind of turned into being mad about the bike. It was like one feeling came on top of the other.
DAN:	I get it. This is going to sound strange, but did you know you can use commas to show one idea coming on top of another? Let me show you. Check out this sentence from "Eleven": "It takes a few days, weeks even, sometimes even months before you say 'eleven' when they ask you."
MAKANI:	Yeah. It's like she's having one thought on top of another about feeling like she's eleven years old. Kind of like waves.
DAN:	Nice. Do you want to try doing something like that in your piece?

Makani began to draft, using commas to show his thoughts building "like waves." (See his piece below.) Later, when he shared his work with the class, he explained, "The commas are to make the reader think about how much I adored that bike. They are sort of like stop-and-think commas."

Makani instantly gets hit by a big blue garbage truck, its big metal bumper startling him. It feels to him as if he is in the air for years; he can see his favorite bike get crushed right in front of him. Makani had that bike since he was five years old. It was a great bike, his dream bike, maybe big enough to last him up to 9th grade or more, and it was getting crushed right before his very eyes.

Teaching Point: Writers can use commas to show ideas or feelings building up, and to provide emphasis.

Once Makani had shared it, the comma-as-craft-tool idea caught on with the rest of the class. In subsequent conferences, I was able to pull out "Eleven" (a fabulous mentor text for varied comma use) with other students to look for ideas. His classmate Iris was taken with the Cisneros sentence, "*You open your eyes and everything's just like yesterday, only it's today.*" When I asked what was special about this comma, she replied, "It kind of stops and leaves you hanging for a moment, and sort of says, "BUUUTT.... It lets you pause for a moment to relate to the first part of the sentence, and then you kind of snap back to reality."

Iris went back to a section of her piece about examining an insect in science class and tried her hand at the "snap-back-to-reality" comma. (See her drafts below.)

Iris's first draft:

> Glad that it's over, Iris casually picks up the cover slip. *Forget about it, Iris. No worries. Almost done with this, then you can scrutinize this putrid insect.* A little pep talk is all she needs to boost herself back up. Without giving much attention, she releases the cover slip, tilted at a 45-degree angle. Unfortunately, instead of landing on top of the slide, it found its way to the floor.

Iris's revised draft, with snap-back-to-reality commas:

> Relieved, Iris casually retrieves the cover slip. *Forget about it, Iris. No worries. Almost done with this, then you can scrutinize this putrid insect.* A little pep talk and motivation is all she needs to boost herself back up, though her spirits aren't quite soaring as before. Without giving much attention, she releases the cover slip, tilted at a 45-degree angle. She expects it to land on top of the slide, only it finds its way to the floor.

Teaching Point: Writers can use commas to contrast opposite ideas or show when something turns out differently than expected.

Yichen, Sixth Grade: Planning for a Beginning, Middle, and Ending (structure)

Children are developmentally wired to live in the moment. This is part of what makes them delightful, but can be frustrating when we are trying to convey the importance of prewriting, or planning out a text.

Yichen is a sixth grader at Shen Wai International School in Shenzhen, China, and a participant in the Ming Yang summer writing workshop. His class had been doing freewrites about their passions, in preparation for writing personal essays.

DAN: So, Yichen, what are you thinking?

YICHEN: I'm thinking about a lot of things. Maybe I want to write about computer games, maybe I want to write about baseball, maybe pizza. *(Laughs.)*

DAN: Whichever you choose, you'll be spending a lot of time writing about it.

YICHEN: I know. So it's got to be worth it. And it's got to not be boring.

DAN: Which do you think would be most interesting for a reader to read about?

YICHEN: Hmm. Probably baseball. It's the most surprising.

DAN: Why? Say more about that.

YICHEN: Because who would think a Chinese kid would like baseball?

DAN: So you'd want your reader to feel surprised. How would you make them feel that?

YICHEN: Probably I should tell the story of how I got interested.

DAN: Would that be the first thing?

YICHEN: I'm not sure. It might need an introduction before that part.

DAN: Yichen, you are on to something important here. Writers think about what specific things will interest a reader in each section. Sounds like you are starting to do that, with the "who-would-think-a-Chinese-kid-would-like-baseball" idea, and how surprising that is. It can be helpful to plan out a piece in three parts before you draft—a beginning, a middle, and an ending—and think about what you want the reader to experience in each part.

YICHEN: Okay, I'll try. The beginning would be talking to the reader, like can you believe it, a Chinese kid likes baseball. Then I can tell the story of how I got interested, which will make them laugh. I'm not sure about the ending, though.

DAN: Here's my suggestion. Why not make a quick chart in your notebook, like this, and fill it out? Not too many words; you'll write the actual piece later. I'll come back in five minutes.

Section	What I'll write	What will interest the reader
Beginning		
Middle		
Ending		

I left Yichen to quickly jot down his ideas, making sure to return before he ran out of steam. Here's what he came up with:

Section	What I'll write	What will interest the reader
Beginning	Talking to the reader, can you believe it	
Middle	Cartoon story, how I got interested	
Ending	What I think now	

Again, in the spirit of listening for the most sophisticated thing a child says or does, I was struck by Yichen's comment about his topic being "surprising." This showed a beginning understanding of taking the reader's perspective. When I asked follow-up questions, Yichen was able to go there as well—though I'm not sure he would have continued to think about it without my encouragement. The planning chart activity served to concretize the idea. I ended the conference by reiterating the teaching point and suggesting it could apply to future pieces as well.

The next day, Yichen turned in this chatty first draft, a nice execution of his plan:

Baseball

I ⭐ You may want to ask, why a Chinese kid will be such a fan of baseball? Well, the story is quite funny, that you won't able to imagine how I get contact with baseball. So making the long story short, I know baseball from a cartoon, yes, a cartoon, called. Doraemon. You will ofcourse be very confused, what is the relationship between baseball and such a cartoon? Well, when I was about 9, I watch Doraemon, it is a Japanese cartoon, so sometimes there are scene of Nobita playing baseball. I found it interesting, so I began to "play" baseball at home with Leon, my yonger brother. Until one day, my mom introduce us the but swinging sport, baseball, and soon she take us. to a baseball lesson, we really like it, so after 3 Years of training, I become what I am now, the second main pitcher of our school-team. Leon, he is fast as a rocket, sometimes even faster than me. He said that he would like to be the catcher, but I think he should be the SS. (short stop), because. he is very fast, but he is small, not that strong, so I think it is better for him to be the SS, and I have evidences, he cant sometime even dare to catch my fast ball.

Teaching Point: Writers can plan their pieces in three parts, thinking ahead about what they want their reader to experience in each section.

Tricks of the Trade: What Do These Conferences Have in Common?

As varied as the writing strategies and individual students were in the preceding conferences, five essential teaching moves were the same. Each of these are critical in helping students become independent writing decision-makers.

Say more about that.

Early on in each conference I listened for comments that suggested a beginning understanding of some aspect of writing, and asked the student to elaborate, or "say more"—sometimes more than once.

This goes back to the principles of listening discussed back in Chapter One—be curious, ask questions. Many teachers feel insecure about singling out the perfect thing to follow up on at this stage, but it's best not to overthink it. Trust your teacher instinct; if a student comment strikes you as interesting, it's probably worth pursuing. In each conference, the teaching point evolved from this follow-up questioning. And just asking lets the child know her thoughts were a key factor in determining the direction of the conference.

Quote the piece and/or the student.

It's one thing to *say* you value someone's ideas; it's another to show it. Leaping straight to a general writing strategy, stated in teacher language, can feel impersonal. Honoring a student's actual words sends the message that this conference could not have happened in exactly the same way for anyone else. "Kids are always amazed when I quote the sentences they wrote in their pieces back to them in a conference," says New York City teacher and coach Tiana Silvas. "They feel pretty important."

Referencing specific parts in children's writing and/or phrases they use to explain their thinking shows you are listening carefully, appreciating their hard work, and (most importantly) allowing co-ownership of the conference.

It's one thing to say you value someone's ideas; it's another to show it.... Honoring a student's actual words sends the message that this conference could not have happened in exactly the same way for anyone else.

Let the student try the new strategy independently before ending the conference.

To be sure that students have internalized what we've taught, it makes sense to have them try implementing it independently before ending a conference. This means walking away and returning a few minutes later to connect what the student has learned to future writing.

As odd as it may seem, this act of walking away is a key move—no one loves being watched the first time they attempt something unfamiliar. Leaving for a few minutes so the student can try the writing strategy on her own allows space for struggle, working through problems, and ultimately a sense of ownership. Not insignificantly, it lets the young writer know that her teacher is confident in her ability to do this new thing independently.

On a logistical level, as Carl Anderson (2019) points out, walking away for a few minutes also allows us to start a new conference, ultimately fitting in more meetings in a single period. Once the last child has tried out the new strategy, returning to wrap up the conference by reiterating the teaching point and relating it to future writing is more meaningful. After all, once a student has done it herself, it's easier to imagine using it elsewhere.

Leaving for a few minutes so the student can try the writing strategy on her own allows space for struggle, working through problems, and ultimately a sense of ownership.

Consider using examples from mentor texts.

Becoming skilled at just about anything usually involves learning from someone who knows how to do it well—a mentor. To learn from such a person involves observing in a particular way—making note of her moves, techniques, and tricks. For a writer, books can be teachers. "When you start reading in a certain way," remarks poet Tess Gallagher (1998), "that's already the beginning of your writing."

One of the most useful skills we can model in a conference is how to read in this "certain way"—looking at how other authors do it. In other words, we want students to look at texts as mentors—*mentor texts*—which can teach us specific things about writing. "Very simply," Allison Marchetti and Rebekah O'Dell write in *A Teacher's Guide to Mentor Texts* (2021), "a mentor text is a text created by a professional that helps us make texts of our own."

For Carrie, looking at the way Kate DiCamillo mixed up long and short sentences helped her figure out how to do it herself. For Makani, considering Sandra Cisneros's use of commas taught him how to look at punctuation differently. Hearing how Ralph Fletcher mixed internal feelings with external action inspired Min to try it in his kangaroo story.

Not every writing conference involves looking at a published example, but it is a good idea to keep a stack of familiar mentor texts at the ready when conferring. At first, this prospect may seem daunting—how to know which books will be most useful to use for teaching a particular writing strategy? Happily, most texts in elementary and middle school libraries are filled with examples of a variety of writing strategies. Class read-alouds are a good starting point, as students are familiar with the content and can look at them more objectively as pieces of writing.

Share individual students' conferring lessons with the rest of the class.

Once students understand that some lessons in writing workshop are for the entire class and some are for individual writers, they naturally become curious about what others are doing. Indeed, conferring at a group table with one writer usually results in her neighbor classmates trying out the new strategy as well. In a few of the preceding sample conferences, having students share what they learned had a ripple effect. Makani's comma discovery got the seventh graders at Taipei International School excited about comma possibilities in a way that a teacher-led lesson would not, and Imani's talking-to-the-reader conference caught on quickly with her fellow second graders in Harlem.

If our objective is for students to become independent writing decision-makers with a range of strategies to choose from, we need to create and nurture a community where children regularly share ideas. A teacher is responsible for explicitly teaching new content, but just as importantly must ensure opportunities for young writers to learn from each other. Share time needn't always be who-tried-what-the-teacher-taught-in-today's-lesson-and-how-did-it-go; sometimes it should be what-can-I-learn-from-my-fellow-writers!

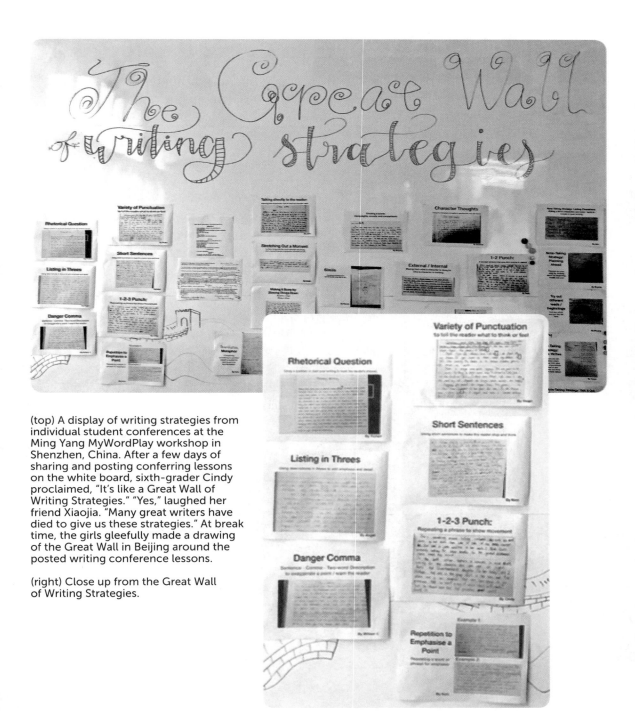

(top) A display of writing strategies from individual student conferences at the Ming Yang MyWordPlay workshop in Shenzhen, China. After a few days of sharing and posting conferring lessons on the white board, sixth-grader Cindy proclaimed, "It's like a Great Wall of Writing Strategies." "Yes," laughed her friend Xiaojia. "Many great writers have died to give us these strategies." At break time, the girls gleefully made a drawing of the Great Wall in Beijing around the posted writing conference lessons.

(right) Close up from the Great Wall of Writing Strategies.

Keeping Track: Note-Taking and Record-Keeping

Continuity is critical in any sort of teaching, and writing conferences are no exception. If every lesson is completely new and unrelated to the one before, making connections and building skills as a writer would be very difficult. It is in a student's interest to extend the previous teaching point for more than one conference. Over time you will sense when it's time to change course and address a different quality of writing.

Approaching each conference as something completely new makes it harder for the grown-up as well. While the idea is always to respond to a child in the moment, thinking ahead about possibilities for extending the previous teaching point often makes the conversation more focused. To that end, keeping a record of past conferences and reviewing it ahead of time can reduce the stress of finding a direction when we sit down with a child.

Writing down important information as a conference progresses also helps us maintain focus and concentrate on the child. "Taking notes grounds me in conferences because I'm less distracted," admits Ryan Scala, a fifth-grade teacher at Spring School in East Hampton, New York. "Teachers have a million plates spinning, and it helps me tune out the white noise. Also, when I'm taking notes it forces me to do less talking and more listening."

There is no one way to take notes in a conference. Some find graphic organizers or spreadsheets (such as the ones in Chapter Three) helpful, while others prefer their own personal shorthand. Whichever method you choose, it's important to record:

- What the student is doing well
- Choice phrases, either from the writing itself or what the student said (don't paraphrase!)
- Teaching point (in transferable language that can apply to future writing)
- Assignment (what the student will do to practice in today's piece)
- Possible next steps

Keeping a record of past conferences and reviewing it ahead of time can reduce the stress of finding a direction when we sit down with a child.

Note-Taking in Action: Arael

Arael is a fifth grader in Ryan Scala's writing workshop. "He is one of the trickier students to confer with because he is already a fairly strong writer," Ryan reflected. "The goals I had for him at the start of the year focused on development, elaboration, and craft. Another goal tied to this was to linger longer in the revision stage. Also punctuating dialogue, and learning how to vary sentence length and craft complex sentences."

The class began the year with a unit on personal narrative, followed by a realistic fiction study. "Since both involved storytelling elements, I was able to segue from one teaching point to another pretty naturally," Ryan explained. "Looking over my notes as I went along helped me stay on course and follow up on ideas from conference to conference."

A look at Ryan's notes illustrates how this unfolded.

Writing Conference Note-Taking Form

Date:	Name: Arael
10/1	**Compliment:** He does a nice job with the internal story (I thought, I wondered). Also, he understands the larger meaning in the story. Describes himself as the kind of writer who paragraphs after drafting. **Teaching Point:** Go back to the part that you were most afraid—STRETCH that out. Use Arael to talk about the ending in SHARE (coach him around endings or mirror write). **Next Step:** Become the kind of writer who thinks in paragraphs, endings. **Quality/Qualities of Writing:** Communicate meaning/Write with detail.
10/8	**Compliment:** Doesn't just capture any moment or just write what happened, but instead tries to write using story structure: problem/resolution, shows how the character's feelings change at the end of the story. **Teaching Point:** Writers of personal narratives revise to bring out how the character felt about the problem by adding what the character did, said, or thought about the problem at different points in the story, not just at the end. **Next Step:** Other ways to elaborate: include physical descriptions of the character, or include flashback or flash forward that connect to meaning. **Quality/Qualities of Writing:** Use genre knowledge/Write with detail.
10/19	**Compliment:** Uses dialogue to affect the pacing of the story, match the tone/mood (scary, suspenseful). **Teaching Point:** Writers realize that the setting can be introduced in their lead just like their characters and so they revise to include details about the setting (heard, saw, weather) in order to create a mood/or tone in the scene. **Next Step:** Writers study mentor texts to find other ways to develop tension in a scene (perhaps a cliffhanger), use different kinds of punctuation (dashes, ellipses), vary sentence length (long/short). **Quality/Qualities of Writing:** Use genre knowledge/write with detail.

Go to page 173 and scholastic.com/RadicalListeningResources for a reproducible/downloadable version of this form.

On October 1, Arael was working on "Waterslide," a personal narrative about his trip to a water park. As reflected in his notes, Ryan scanned the piece in progress and noticed some inner thinking ("He does a nice job with the internal story"), and learned from Arael that he "is the kind of writer who thinks about paragraphs after drafting." (See draft below.) Leveraging the nascent understanding of going inside a narrator's head, Ryan chose as a teaching point stretching out the emotional part, e.g., when he "was most afraid."

Arael   October 1, 2020

WaTeRsLiDe

Alfonso turns to my cousin, Jeremy, and says, " Let's go on this one"

"Ok sure!" He said. I look up at the slide, it looks REALLY BIG. I had butterflies in my stomach, and I thought to myself that PHEW - This slide is SUPER TALL. I'm not really sure I want to go on it, I thought by second guessing myself. I didn't say a word, palms sweaty and got all quiet.

Step by step, higher and higher as we went up the stairs. More people forming the line and I thought to myself, well there's no going back now. Once we were slowly approaching the top you can see the whole waterpark and all the little people looking like little ants when you pick up a rock.

After having Arael think aloud about how and where this might go, Ryan left him to work independently. A few days later, he had revised his draft and added a full new paragraph, describing his fear in detail. (See his revised draft on the next page.)

> Arael   October 5, 2020
>
> **WaTeRsLiDe**
>
> Alfonso turns to my cousin, Jeremy, and says, "<u>Let's</u> go on this one"
>
> "Ok sure!" He said. I look up at the slide, it looks REALLY BIG. I had butterflies in my stomach, and I thought to myself that PHEW - This slide is SUPER TALL. I'm not really sure I want to go on it, I thought by second guessing myself. I didn't say a word, palms sweaty and got all quiet.
>
> Every little step I took the more nervous and creak by creak seeing the people in front of us swooshing down splashing every single person and each step I took felt like ten more butterflies appeared in my stomach. <u>Also</u> at the same time trying not to look down and see how bad it would be if I fell.
>
> I wondered what if something went wrong? Step by step, higher and higher as we went up the stairs. More people forming the line and I thought to myself, well there's no going back now. Once we were slowly approaching the top you can see the whole waterpark and all the little people looking like little ants when you pick up a rock.

"When it was time for our next conference a week later," Ryan explained, "I looked over my notes and thought about how to extend the teaching point from last time. What Arael had said about paragraphs was interesting, how he adds them after drafting, so I asked about that. He told me he thinks about story structure—problem and resolution, and summing up the character's feelings at the end. In that moment I realized he could try stretching out the big feeling parts all through the different sections of the piece—putting the elaboration idea together with his starting to think about parts of a story. So that became the teaching point."

Arael ultimately turned in a revised draft with stretched-out internal feeling sprinkled throughout the piece. (See revised draft on the next page.) "As I was wrapping up that conference, it occurred to me a next step might be to teach him to elaborate in other ways besides internal thinking. So at the end of the period, I added that to my notes."

Arael   October 9, 2020

WaTeRsLiDe

Alfonso turns to my cousin, Jeremy, and says, "Let's go on this one"

"Ok sure!" He said. I look up at the slide, it looks REALLY BIG. I had butterflies in my stomach, and I thought to myself that PHEW - This slide is SUPER TALL. I'm not really sure I want to go on it, I thought by second guessing myself. I didn't say a word, palms sweaty and got all quiet.

Every little step I took the more nervous and creak by creak seeing the people in front of us swooshing down splashing every single person and each step I took felt like ten more butterflies appeared in my stomach. Also at the same time trying not to look down and see how bad it would be if I fell.

I wondered what if something went wrong? Step by step, higher and higher as we went up the stairs. More people forming the line and I thought to myself, well there's no going back now. Once we were slowly approaching the top you can see the whole waterpark and all the little people looking like little ants when you pick up a rock.

When we got to the top there was a person blowi[ng] all chose a number to lay in, and I walked slowly over, g[...] laid down with my mat in my row. As all the other peopl[e...] the slide, the water rushing down lumps and seeing the g[...]

bottom. And for a moment I was so nervous that my heart felt like it was beating 100 miles an hour. I was also eyeing the person that worked there and seeing his whistle slowly going in his mouth and him looking back up to us and seeing if we were ready. And also that is when I felt like I haven't eaten anything for hours, when I just ate something not that long ago. My stomach felt so empty that's how anxious I felt. Then I said to my cousin next to me " This is so much bigger than from the bottom,"

"Yea I know." he said.

And then when we were all ready and in position the man said "3, 2, 1, WSHH" and we all pushed off, going so fast I was so nervous.

But then suddenly almost arriving at the end I thought to myself there's nothing to be nervous about this is really fun.

After when we arrived at the end I asked my cousin "Wanna go again" and he said "Yea it was so fun."

Then I looked up at something I was once scared of not that long ago. Also looking over to some of the other big slides that were the size of this one and seeing that there is nothing to be nervous about and that I can do this and anything that I put my mind to.

About 10 days later, the class was working on realistic fiction, and Arael opted to try his hand at a scary story. Scanning the writing, Ryan noted his use of dialogue right away ("Uses dialogue to affect the pacing of the story, tone/mood"). Being conscious of the mood of a story was a new element in the mix, so Ryan chose to wed this insight with his next step idea from last time ("...other ways to elaborate"). "Since he was already thinking about story elements, which I remembered when looking over my notes," Ryan explained, "it would make sense to go there. But at the same time I wanted it to be something concrete, which I was sure he'd be successful with. So I went for ledes and setting. I had him say a few possibilities out loud, and left him to it." When Ryan returned a few minutes later, Arael had already revised his draft:

The Light In The Room   10/28/20

by Arael

It was a cold breezy night when four friends stumbled across an old scary house. When they all decided to go in they walked up to the house and Max said "It smells terrible here."

"Yeah it stinks," says Tristan.

Then suddenly the door shut behind them and Steven tried to open it. Then he said "Guys it's locked." And they got really nervous.

Jack said "Guys what if we are trapped here forever?"

What Can We Learn From Ryan's Conference Notes?

Looking over Ryan's conference notes and Arael's writing, a few things stand out. First, his writing is far from perfect. There are punctuation lapses and errors in tense. At the same time, Arael is clearly growing as a writer. His use of elaboration techniques is becoming more sophisticated, and there is a developing understanding of mood and setting.

It is tempting when sitting down with a young writer to correct the mistakes and perfect the piece of writing. The problem is when the teacher is the one doing the fixing, the student doesn't learn to make her own writing decisions. As Lucy Calkins (1994) memorably advised, "(We) are teaching the writer, not the writing. Our decisions must be guided by what might help this writer, rather than what might help this writing."

Ryan's savvy use of conferring notes served multiple purposes. As he mentioned, the act of concentrating on the child's words and scanning the work allowed him to "tune out the white noise," and notice things that might not otherwise have been apparent. At the same time, when students see us taking what they say seriously enough to write it down, they feel their thoughts are valued and often think more deeply.

This win-win dynamic has benefits beyond one conference. Even a teacher with a photographic memory will likely not remember everything that comes up in a conferring conversation from one week to the next. While looking over his notes from October 1, Ryan was struck with Arael's comment about paragraphs, and used that as a jumping-off point for spreading out elaboration across sections. That in turn led to Arael talking about story structure on October 8, which led to the lesson on introducing setting in the lede of a story.

When students see us taking what they say seriously enough to write it down, they feel their thoughts are valued and often think more deeply.

Apart from connecting conference A to conference B, there are longer-term benefits to note-taking as well. "Every time I meet with a student, writing goals for the future occur to me that might not fit with that day's conference," explains Ryan. "As I log in more and more conferences with a single kid, I have more and more potential teaching points in my head to go to with that student when it feels appropriate."

Though a writing conference involves reacting in the moment, it is a mistake to think of conferring as a completely spontaneous exercise. Careful note-taking allows us to look for openings and opportunities to address long-term goals in subsequent conferences. The nice thing is, even if the teaching point doesn't arise out of something that happened that day, it can still relate back to something the student said or did previously. And the truth is, when we say to a young writer, "I'm thinking back to that thing you said three weeks ago," it sends a powerful message about the power of listening. After all, how often does a teacher remember (and validate) a child's exact words so long after the fact?

CHAPTER FIVE

Connecting Reading and Writing Conferences

*"The writer and the reader stand at either end of a pond.
The writer drops a pebble in and the ripples reach the reader.
The writer stands there, imagining the way the reader is receiving
those ripples, by way of deciding which pebble to drop in next.
Meanwhile, the reader receives those ripples and, somehow,
they speak to her. In other words, they're in connection."*

—George Saunders

Courtney and Noor move from reading to writing and back again in their virtual conference.

"Hi, Noor! We are here today to talk about your reading *and* your writing. So which do you want to talk about first?"

In Courtney Al Moreno's seventh-grade humanities class at the American Embassy School in New Delhi, India, the line separating reading and writing workshop is not always distinct. Especially when she is conferring, a lesson can often go back and forth between the two.

Noor doesn't miss a beat. "My writing. Well, both, sort of," she corrects herself. "In one of my favorite books—actually it's a whole series of books—they're written from all the different characters' perspectives. I really like that idea of seeing both perspectives. Because you can feel like you're actually living there, right there, with each character, throughout every moment. That's what I love in a book, so I'm putting what I love into my fiction writing."

This natural back and forth between the two subjects is not an anomaly in Courtney's class. It's part of the daily discourse. But making the reading-writing connection is just the first step. The next step is what you do with it.

"So you're thinking about the perspective piece," Courtney continues, pushing Noor further. "What does that look like? Can you say more about that?"

Noor pauses for a minute. "Well, I was thinking about how last week you told us when there was trouble in relationships in the books we're reading, we couldn't just say, 'Oh *he's* being a jerk and that's why she's mad.' We had to look at why he was being a jerk, why something was happening. And that's a lot like what I'm doing in my story."

"Okay, so then what?" Courtney digs deeper, confident her student will follow. "Can you give me specifics?"

"Everyone has a story," Noor purses her lips as she works to articulate her thinking. "Everyone comes from somewhere. Nothing is just 'cause fate decided it. Something has to influence an action for it to happen."

Courtney brings it back to the concrete. "So what's the work you want to do to bring those different perspectives front and center in your story?"

Noor pivots to a recent reading experience. "When I started reading Harry Potter, you said J.K. Rowling planned out every little detail. At first, I was like, why would you do that? You can just write! And now I get it because I see you have to plan out every single detail. It was the last project we did that really made me understand that because I was looking to see how writers sprinkle characteristics throughout their writing. And that made me realize you have to plan out every characteristic before you rush into making a story."

Courtney takes the opportunity to connect today's conference to an earlier one. "I love hearing you say that! So now I want to get you thinking about how that might work. Can I give you a teaching point?" Noor nods. "At our last meeting, you were talking about developing the theme of your story, and now you are talking about perspective. Today I want to teach you that authors—like yourself— use characters' perspectives to push their themes forward. When you think about their different points of view, why they do what they do, you can use that to bring out your theme."

Character	What they are feeling	why?
Karina	Karina thinks that Chris is one of the jerks.	In sixth grade, he laughed with everyone else at her when her name was on the 'girls with the hairiest arms' list.
Chris	Chris doesn't know what to say to Karina, but he notices her, and wants to apologise but doesn't know how.	Chris has worked hard for his 'social status' and if he stands up for Karina he is afraid he'll lose it all. This I can understand, belonging has always been a huge need for me. Chris knows that it's wrong but doesn't know what to do about it.

Noor's planning chart

Courtney and Noor agree on an assignment; Noor will create a perspective planning chart and think ahead about what her main characters are feeling, and why. In the "why?" column, she will articulate the themes reflected in the character's actions. (See her chart at left.)

Largely without prompting, this 12-year-old deftly moves from writing to reading and back again, as though nothing could be more logical. How did she get there?

Teaching Point: One way a reader can identify multiple themes in a book is by paying attention to the perspectives of different characters. A writer can express different themes in her story by planning out the individual points of view of her characters.

Why Connect Reading and Writing?

Reading is essential for learning to write, and writing is essential for deepening our reading comprehension.

Asked his advice for aspiring writers, American novelist William Faulkner advised, "Read, read, read. Read everything—trash, classics, good and bad, and see how they do it. Just like a carpenter who works as an apprentice and studies the master."

It isn't only the learning of writing strategies that comes out of looking at author's craft. "Reading like a writer can help strengthen your skills in communication and storytelling," suggests a 2020 article from CNBC's website. "The takeaway here is that writers use words that are deeply tied to human senses—words that "come to life" in the reader's mind. Reading like a writer can help you understand their tools and craft, which can be used to your advantage in real-life situations, no matter what field of work you're in."

The idea that reading about something makes it come to life in our minds isn't just speculation. "The brain, it seems," according to the neurological studies at the University of Toronto, as reported in *The New York Times* (2012), "does not make much of a distinction between reading about an experience and encountering it in real life. In each case the same neurological regions are stimulated." Authors, educators, philosophers, neurologists—all agree the two processes are intrinsically linked.

But before we get into the nuts and bolts of the implications for teaching practice, it's worth thinking about another reason to teach reading and writing connections: empathy.

In the epigraph at the beginning of this chapter, George Saunders (2021) beautifully describes a writer and a reader as standing "at either end of a pond." He goes on to caution that "Those two people, in those postures, across that pond, are doing essential work. This is not a hobby, pastime, or indulgence. By their mutual belief in connection, they're making the world better, by making it (at least between the two of them, in that small moment) more friendly. We might even say they're preparing for future disaster; when disaster comes, they'll enter it with a less panicky, reactive vision of the Other, because they've spent so much time in connection with an imaginary Other, while reading or writing."

Another master American novelist, Toni Morrison, approaches empathy differently. "When I taught creative writing at Princeton, [my students] had been told all of their lives to write what they knew. I always began the course by saying, 'Don't pay any attention to that. Think of somebody you don't know. What about a Mexican waitress in the Rio Grande who can barely speak English? Or what about a Grande Madame in Paris? Things way outside their camp. Imagine it, create it....' I was always amazed at how effective that was.... Even if they ended up just writing an autobiography, at least they could relate to themselves as strangers" (2014).

In the day-to-day life of a classroom, we must be on the lookout for specific points of connection—and be prepared to point them out to students as we confer.

Clearly, teaching children is different from teaching graduate students. But the essential takeaway is when we write, we put ourselves in someone else's head, at least for a moment—be it a character we are trying to create or a reader we are hoping to convince. And when we read, we enter into the mind of the writer, trying to understand what she is saying and where she is coming from.

Thus, the acts of reading and writing can be thought of as reciprocal exercises in empathy—in entertaining other perspectives, however briefly. And when conscientious teachers embrace that idea, making reading-writing connections can be a step in the direction of helping children understand other human beings.

*

This all makes sense, in theory. But in the day-to-day life of a classroom, how do we make these connections clear to young readers and writers? As I mentioned in Chapter One, individual conferences provide powerful opportunities to make reading and writing connections explicit. But for us to take advantage of those opportunities, we must be on the lookout for specific points of connection—and be prepared to point them out to students as we confer.

Qualities of Writing and Reading Comprehension Strategies: Opportunities for Connection

In a writing conference, it's essential to know the qualities of writing and be able to explain them in a general, transferable way. It's also critical for the student to feel a sense of ownership and try out new strategies—with scaffolding and then independently (see Chapter Four). When it's the teacher alone making suggestions and corrections, it's more about "fixing" the single piece of writing than teaching the child.

Similarly, in a reading conference, we must first be familiar with the content of comprehension—both what readers do in their heads to make meaning (metacognition), and what's on the page (text-based). Again, our role is to recognize entry points for teaching which come from what a student is noticing, and help her go deeper (see Chapter Three).

Knowing where and how those two bodies of content knowledge meet is the key to teaching children to make meaningful reading and writing connections. Though it's not an exact science, it can be a helpful exercise when teaching something specific about reading to consider its mirror image in writing, and when teaching something specific about writing to consider its mirror image in reading. For example, to decide where to elaborate and add detail, a writer must first determine what's important—prioritizing, in reading lingo. Figuring out a piece's structure means thinking about the best way to make sections connect, aka synthesis. When a reader feels sad or visualizes a scene, she is evoking sensory and emotional images by paying attention to an author's craft moves. Even conventions, usually thought of as merely a set of rules, can be used to create suspense or to prioritize ideas—which could be pointed out in a reading conference.

And those are just a few examples.

Points of Connection

Qualities of Writing	Comprehension Strategies
Elaboration/Detail	Determining Importance
Structure/Organization	Synthesis
Craft/Voice	Inference Evoking Sensory Images
Conventions	Determining Importance Evoking Sensory Images

Teaching these connections need not always be planned for. In fact, there's something powerful about bringing them up spontaneously. Courtney Al Moreno, a case in point, never misses an opportunity to reference reading while teaching writing, which results in the Noors of the world doing the same. "I find when something becomes part of the daily discourse," she asserts, "kids pick up on your cues. The nice thing is they start coming up with observations on their own. When they do, I make sure to name them so they stick. Sometimes my students' observations are better than mine!" At other times, of course, we want to be more intentional and design explicit lessons about reading like a writer and writing like a reader.

Conferring allows us to find entry points for individual children where a specific reading-writing connection might be helpful. Two ways to shine a light on such connections might be:

- to address parallel teaching points across reading and writing conferences.
- to address reading and writing teaching points in the same conference.

Let's look at each of those possibilities.

Addressing Parallel Teaching Points Across Reading and Writing Conferences

Whether it's a reading or writing conference, we want to take our cue from the student. But this is not a passive exercise on the teacher's part; sometimes it means actively pointing out a connection the child would be unlikely to see on her own. It isn't taking away ownership to begin a writing conference by asking a student to consider the mirror strategy she discussed at her last reading conference. For example, we might say, "I'm thinking about what you said in our last reading conference about noticing strong feeling parts in your book. Are you thinking about where you want your reader to infer feelings in the piece *you* are writing?"

Whether it's a reading or writing conference, we want to take our cue from the student. But this is not a passive exercise on the teacher's part; sometimes it means actively pointing out a connection the child would be unlikely to see on her own.

What follows is a chart with some parallel teaching points to suggest how a teacher might follow up a reading conference in writing—and vice versa.

A FEW PARALLEL (MIRROR) TEACHING POINTS FOR READING CONFERENCES

If in a reading conference, a student:	...in the next writing conference, you might:	Possible questions (depending on what the student does or doesn't notice):
...talks about how one part of the text makes her think back to something from an earlier section... (Synthesis)	...ask where she wants to include "think backward" parts in her piece. (Structure/Craft)	• "Where do you want to remind your reader of something from earlier in the piece? How can you do that without repeating what you said before? Let's look at how your author does it." • "When you read that 'think backward' part in your book, does it help you guess what might happen next? Do you imagine 'think backward' parts can sometimes lead to 'think forward' parts?"
...is thinking about what details are more and less important... (Prioritizing)	...ask which details she most wants her reader to pay attention to, and where she might put them in the piece so they register as important. (Structure)	• "What do you notice about the types of things the writer chose to include?" • "What sorts of things do you imagine she could have included, but chose to leave out?" • "If you wrote this text, what would you have left out or included? Why?" • "How can you make sure your reader understands which details are most (and least) important?"
...is noticing how the mood of the story (or the feelings of a character) changes... (Evoking Sensory and Emotional Images/ Inference)	...work on details that establish a mood (e.g., facial expressions, character actions, setting descriptions, etc.). (Craft/Voice)	• "Where would you say the mood of the story changes? How do you know? Can you point to a specific place where you noticed it was different?" • "What do you imagine caused the character's feelings to change? Where did that happen?" • "What would someone's face look like if they felt that way? How would you describe it? Can you add that to your piece?" • "How would you describe the setting in such a way that it makes your reader feel sad/ happy/excited?"
...points out how some parts are "boring" or confusing, but others are more interesting... (Monitor for Meaning)	...work on varying sentence types, or experimenting with punctuation, for clarity. (Conventions)	• "Let's look at which parts in your book are confusing. Is there anything those parts have in common? Which parts are clearer?" • "One thing authors do to make their writing more interesting is to mix long and short sentences. Are all of your sentences the same length?"

A FEW PARALLEL (MIRROR) TEACHING POINTS FOR WRITING CONFERENCES

If in a writing conference, a student:	...in the next reading conference you might:	Possible questions (depending on what the student does or doesn't notice):
...is deciding which parts need more detail and which parts need less... (Elaboration)	...suggest she study where her author adds more or less detail, and why. (Prioritizing)	• "Where in the story/article are the most important details? How did you know they were important?" • "Which parts did the author spend the most/least time on, and why?" • "In which parts of your piece will you include the most/least detail? Let's plan it out together."
...is deciding which sections should go first, last, etc.... (Structure)	...examine how the sections of her text connect and build. (Synthesis)	• "What would be the best way to begin your piece to get your reader interested? Which information would make the most sense to put next?" • "Where would you say your author ended one section and moved to the next? How did your author let you know?" • "Let's look at how your author made transitions from one section to the next. Can you try that in your piece?"
...is working on drafting dialogue... (Craft/ Conventions)	...notice the sort of character information her author puts in the dialogue, and/ or how dialogue and description combine to create a scene. (Evoking Sensory and Emotional Images/Inference)	• "What other words besides 'said' does the author use to show who is talking? What sort of information about the character's feelings do we learn from these words?" • "What are you trying to show about the character's relationship through this dialogue?" • "Does your author mix any other sentences in during the dialogue? What sorts of descriptions does she put in?"
...is adding sensory detail (e.g., how things look, sound, feel, etc.)... (Elaboration/Craft)	...pay special attention to parts that make a reader visualize a scene. (Inference)	• "Where are some places in your book that make a movie in your mind? How does the author do that?" • "Where are some places that don't make a movie in your mind? What do you do in your head in those parts?" • "Authors sprinkle sensory description all through a piece of writing. Where would the best place be to include it in your piece?"

Addressing Reading and Writing Teaching Points in the Same Conference

In most schools, reading workshop and writing workshop are treated as separate, distinct components. While it's certainly true there are different lessons to be learned in each, it's worth considering how to make them feel less separate if we want students to make connections across reading and writing. Ellin Keene has suggested the idea of a "literacy studio," where children get to choose the subject they'd like to concentrate on each day. "For many, it's the optimal arrangement for two reasons," she explains. "First, the student-based reason. Kids don't automatically make connections between how a reading skill is relevant in writing and vice versa. For example, images—a kid who is visualizing in reading won't automatically think about how to do that as a writer, if we don't make the connection explicit in lessons or in conferences. Then there's the teacher-based reason: time efficiency. You save time when there's a dual focus on reading and writing in the same mini-lesson." In a literacy studio model, some teachers choose to maintain this double focus every day, while others opt to use it a day or two a week, and keep the workshops separate on other days.

Whether the two workshops are taught separately or in tandem, when we meet individually with a student there are myriad possibilities for making connections. Sometimes a conference that starts out about reading naturally gravitates to writing. Other times the conversation ends up crossing both subject areas. When we consistently draw parallels between the two throughout the day, students naturally begin to do so as well. (Just look at Noor, at the beginning of this chapter.)

Not every conference need be (nor should be!) a hybrid reading-writing moment. But when we leave ourselves open to the possibility, individual meetings with students often present golden opportunities for such connections.

Some ideas:

- a writing conference where we plan for places we want a reader to *infer*
- a reading conference where we examine an author's punctuation decisions
- a writing conference where we study and imitate aspects of a favorite author's style (e.g., sensory descriptions, chapter beginnings and endings, etc.)
- a reading conference where we focus on the effect an author creates by varying sentence lengths

What follows are partial transcripts of a few real-life hybrid conferences, annotated along the way.

Eva, Sixth Grade: A Reader Studies an Author's Craft Moves

Eva, a student at Oyster River Middle School in Durham, New Hampshire, is an avid reader and writer. Her ELA teacher, Emily Geltz, routinely uses her own writing as a teaching tool, modeling the way she makes decisions by seeing things through the eyes of a reader.

Going in, both Eva and I assumed we would be talking exclusively about her reading. But as will become evident, the conversation took another turn.

DAN: So, Eva. You are reading Laurie Halse Anderson's *Forge*. *(Eva nods.)* Ms. Geltz tells me you are the sort of reader who really likes plot twists. Can you tell me a little about that?

EVA: I just like it because it keeps me in the book. I don't like a book that just drops in the middle, 'cause then I don't feel the urge to keep reading.

DAN: How do you feel when you come to those parts?

EVA: Well, my mom and I are reading *Forge*, and when there's a plot twist or a cliffhanger at the end of a chapter my mom is like, "Okay, we're all done for the night," and I'm like "No! We need to read more! More!"

DAN: I'm getting the feeling you are an emotional reader. Tell me about that.

EVA: Yeah, some books do make me feel strongly about some things.

Here, early on, I've asked Eva to "say more" about three specific things—why she likes plot twists, how it feels when she gets to those parts, and her experience as an emotional reader. But these questions didn't come from nowhere. As the conversation began to unfold, I listened for the most interesting part of each response, then asked her to say more about *that*. A bit like uncovering the layers of an onion!

Next, I invited Eva to be more specific—first about the idea of strong feeling parts in general, then regarding an example in the book she was reading that day.

DAN: I'm guessing that not every part in every book makes you have a strong feeling. Can you tell me about the kinds of parts that do?

EVA: Well, in books like this, when authors introduce something the reader hasn't had an insight on. If they introduce something that is new to everybody and then just drop it in, that makes me angry, kind of—like I want to read more.

DAN: So some of these parts are places where the author is making you feel a certain way. Do you think that's in you, or is Laurie Halse Anderson doing that on purpose?

EVA: I think that she's doing it on purpose. Definitely.

DAN: Interesting. Can you show me a part where Laurie manipulated your feelings?

EVA: I'll try to find it. *(Flips through pages.)* This part! *(Points.)* All these long paragraphs, and then this one-sentence paragraph: "James Billingham had come to camp."

DAN: What's up with that?

EVA: I think the reason it made me feel that way is because the main character, Curzon, who was a slave? His old master has come back. So he thinks he may have strong feelings against him. I was surprised, and a lot of things hit me, a lot of inferences and predictions about what might happen, because I didn't trust this guy. I didn't know if he would be dishonest.

Though so far we'd been mostly talking about *Forge*, our conversation centered on *what the author was doing to make the reader feel a certain way*—a reading like a writer angle. Now it was time to narrow the focus and create an inquiry project that bridged the gap between reading and writing. Eva was only too happy to go there.

DAN: So it sounds like what she's doing as a writer here is manipulating you by getting all descriptive, descriptive, descriptive, then boom—simple. That's kind of interesting.

EVA: I know, yeah. Like all of a sudden, get to the point.

DAN: I have an idea. Since you are clearly the sort of reader who notices how authors do tricks with their writing to manipulate a reader's feelings, how would you like to do a Laurie Halse Anderson manipulating feelings study?

EVA: THAT would be really cool.

DAN: You just came up with one example right here *(Dan marks with a sticky note)*, where she built up and built up and then suddenly went simple. That made you go, "Oh my gosh."

EVA: I need more!

DAN: Do you think that's the only writer's trick she uses to manipulate your feelings?

EVA: No. There have to be others.

After negotiating the parameters of the assignment (due date, how many examples), Eva volunteered that once she had come up with a list of Laurie Halse Anderson's "writer's tricks" for manipulating a reader's feelings, she would apply them to her own writing. (See her list on the next page.) Whenever possible, it is a good idea for the student to take an active role in defining the purpose for her conferring work, even beyond the immediate assignment.

Teaching Point: Parts in books that give a reader a strong feeling keep us engaged and are usually very important to the story. Writers have a variety of ways to craft those parts·to keep the reader "needing more."

Forge by Laurie Halse Anderson

1.   **Page 14, Chapter 2, Paragraph 4**
In this part, Mrs. Anderson used fast-paced, gruesome descriptions to make a reader's stomach churn, and beg for more! I had so many thoughts when I read this part, that it was overwhelming, but if I had to pick one sentence to describe it, it would be: *What* just happened?! My face looked exactly like my mom's, which leads me to think Mrs. Anderson dived deep into those descriptions to make me feel grossed out (and scared, and sad, and *gasp*, and *gag* etc.), so I'd want to read more. It was very suspenseful, and that's exactly what I love!

2.   **Page 173, Chapter 36, Paragraph 14-15**
Mrs. Anderson brings back an important character (known from <u>Chains</u>) with a flourish... then drops the plot into the black hole known as "the end of part 3". Unfortunately, my mom *had* to stop reading at this point, so I practically had to stay up half the night itching to read more. I also think Mrs. Anderson cuts the part off like this to manipulate the reader's' feelings, to make them want to read more.

3.   **Page 207, Chapter , Paragraph 13**
This part caused mom to gasp, which about summed up my feelings. I think Mrs. Anderson adds in this shocking gesture to knock both Curzon and the reader off their feet. Any doubts of hatred for Bellingham are IMMEDIATELY dismissed and the feeling of sympathy for the furious yet stoic Isabel grows. It illustrates that Bellingham views Isabel as solely as an object he owns.

4.   **Page 6, Chapter 1, Paragraph 1-2**
You would expect a gradual beginning, right? If you're reading <u>Forge</u>, after having read <u>Chains</u>, that is NOT the case. This book begins with a firecracker, introducing Isabel's betrayal, but from Curzon's point of view. Mrs. Anderson took my assumptions as a reader and turned them upside down to form a whole new unexpected predicament for Curzon.

Eva's list of Laurie Halse Anderson's "writer's tricks"

Charlotte, Fourth Grade: A Writer Plans for Inference

This conference took place in teacher Tiana Silvas's fourth-grade writing workshop at Public School 59 in New York City. Tiana told me that Charlotte had a good understanding of story structure and often commented on writers' craft moves in her books. Though Charlotte is a strong student, a longer-term goal for her was speaking more metacognitively about what she was doing in her head as a reader. With this information in mind, I began the conference hoping to find a way to leverage these strengths to address her goal.

DAN: Charlotte, you are working on historical fiction, right?

CHARLOTTE: Yes. My writing piece is about the Great Depression. It's about these two girls; when they were going to a train, one got left behind and one got on. I named the girl who got the train Hope, and used her good luck bracelet as symbolism, like her name, Hope. I used that because the book Ms. Tiana gave me, *Bud, Not Buddy*, had a meaningful name behind it, and this book *Call Me Hope* had a meaningful name, too—so I wanted to use that in my writing, too.

Even though we were in writing workshop, Charlotte referenced two books right away. If a teacher remains on the lookout for such moments, there can be natural opportunities to steer the conversation to the overlap between reading comprehension strategies and qualities of writing.

DAN: Interesting. It sounds like you know about things like symbolism, and putting something in a piece of writing that stands for something else. I want to ask you about something. When you read, often you have to read between the lines.

CHARLOTTE: Yes. You mean inference?

DAN: Exactly. It sounds like you are working on inference as a writer. Can you tell me about that?

CHARLOTTE: Well, I know you can't just add something that's not meaningful. You have to have a purpose behind your story. And this is my first time writing historical fiction, so I kind of like want to up my, you know, my game.

DAN: I'm curious about this inference as a writer thing, because everyone always talks about inference as a reader. It seems to me, and I'm curious to know what you think about this, that writers need to plan for their inference. In other words, think about places where they want their reader to understand something they're not exactly saying. Like the symbolism with your good luck charm.

To freeze-frame these last moves, I took care to first mention things I knew Charlotte understood on an emergent level (symbolism, inference) and pushed her to think about them in a way she hadn't considered before: inference as a writer. To introduce this rather sophisticated concept, it made sense to move from the abstract to the concrete, e.g., stating the idea as a general concept ("writers think about places where they want their reader to understand something they're not exactly saying") and then referring to her specific piece ("Like the symbolism with your good luck charm").

Again, it's all about moving from the general to the specific—and back again.

CHARLOTTE: Yeah, it's going to start making a bigger impact as I go along.

DAN: Oh, it's going to come back later, too?

CHARLOTTE: Yeah. I also noticed in *Bud, Not Buddy* that he had this suitcase. He didn't talk every second about it, but at some points he says, "Don't touch it, it's really fragile." And that shows he's using it to kind of keep his parents there, 'cause his dad left when he was a baby, and then his mom died. So he kind of keeps them inside of there, and he's really fragile about anybody touching it. I like how it's sort of slowly coming in, the suitcase, to show you that.

DAN: I imagine that author thought ahead about the places the suitcase was going to come, planned out those places he wanted the reader to infer. And that repetition, having them come up more than once, makes it even more powerful, as you said! I have a suggestion of something you could try. Ms. Tiana told me you are really good with structure, and planning out your pieces. But I'm going to guess you've never planned out your inferences.

CHARLOTTE: Sure, I can work on that. I can plan it out in my writing notebook. I think that would be great for me 'cause I've seen every writer do this, so I want to do it, too.

DAN: What would be the best way to plan your inferences?

CHARLOTTE: Maybe I could do an inference timeline.

In this last exchange, Charlotte began verbally planning how she wanted her piece to go by thinking about her independent book, *Bud, Not Buddy*. I seized the moment to again reference something I knew she understood— structure—and pushed her to go further, connecting it to a reading strategy (inference). Since her class has been exposed to lots of ways to represent their thinking, Charlotte was able to come up with a method for planning her inference independently, using a timeline.

Sounds a bit complicated when you break it down, but as this transcript shows, it flowed very naturally in the conference. It's this sort of cross-pollination that starts to come up naturally when teachers such as Tiana consistently draw parallels between reading and writing in their daily instruction.

Teaching Point: Readers infer things in books through symbols and repeated events. Writers can plan ahead for places where they want their readers to infer.

Nathan, Fourth Grade: A Reader Reflects on an Author's Punctuation

Nathan, a student at Taipei American School, is one of those fourth graders who is always ready with a joke. His teacher described him as a "fan of realistic and action fiction who comes up with great observations in class discussions, but tends to rush his written work. I'd like to see him slow down."

Though it started as a reading conference, as our conversation progressed, things took a different turn.

DAN: I see you are reading *Chasing the Falconers*.

NATHAN: Yeah. It's part of a series.

DAN: Is this your first Gordon Korman book?

NATHAN: No, he's one of my favorite authors. He has a good mix of action and funny, which are the two things I like in books.

DAN: Nice. How exactly does he mix action and funny?

NATHAN: I have no idea.

DAN: I have a suggestion. What if you find a part where it's got action and funny, and we try to figure it out?

NATHAN: Okay. *(Flips through book, stops.)* Got one right here. *(Reads aloud.)*

> Trapped in a boxcar.
>
> Something frantic rattled **around** in Aiden's head. He should know about this! This **was familiar.**
>
> *That's crazy! You've never been on a train that wasn't a commuter. What do you know about escaping from a freight car?*

It's worth noting that when I asked a more abstract question (i.e., *How do you think he does that?*), Nathan's first reaction was to duck it. Again, most nine-year-olds—even deep thinkers like Nathan—tend to be less comfortable without something concrete to sink their teeth into. Asking for an example seemed to open him up and build confidence. When I returned to my line of questioning, he didn't miss a beat.

DAN: Okay, so what do you think? What does Gordon Korman do as a writer to combine action and funny?

NATHAN: Well...it's kind of the way he writes his sentences. They're all weird.

DAN: Can you say more about that?

NATHAN: Yeah. It's like he starts with this really short sentence. Then he gets all action-y.

DAN: What makes it get action-y?

NATHAN: Exclamation points. And then he talks to himself. And more exclamation points. And a question mark!

DAN: Quite a list. When he does all that, what does it make you feel as a reader?

NATHAN: Impressed. It's kind of like they all work together, the sentences. But I think it's mostly the punctuation.

DAN: You mean the exclamation points?

NATHAN: Not just the exclamation points. Also, the short sentences. That's punctuation, too; he puts the full stop in and it makes him sound kind of funny. Ironic.

DAN: Ironic?

NATHAN: Yeah. It sounds like he can't believe what he's got himself into.

DAN: Hmm. You mean you can hear his tone of voice in your head?

NATHAN: Exactly.

DAN: Interesting. So mixing up the different types of sentences, short and long, with different punctuation, creates a feeling of action plus funny. Do you think you can bring this to your writing? After all, you like funny and action, and here Gordon Korman is teaching you how to do that.

NATHAN: Definitely. Never thought of that before.

A closer look at this exchange shows I asked for elaboration—some form of clarification, or *say more about that*—at least five separate times. While responding, Nathan went from "...it's kind of the way he writes his sentences. They're all weird," to "Not just the exclamation points. Also, the short sentences. That's punctuation, too; he puts the full stop in and it makes him sound kind of funny. Ironic... like he can't believe what he's got himself into."

Quite a leap, just from that simple move.

Once there, I named what we had noticed ("So mixing up the different types of sentences, short and long, with different punctuation, creates a feeling of action plus funny.") and made the link to his writing. To follow up, I gave Nathan a graphic organizer from a punctuation inquiry study and asked him to memorialize his observations. He wrote: "I like how he started with a short sentence: trapped in a box car. It makes his voice sound flat, but funny: ironic also the '!' So loud with a '?' at the end. I call this the ironic argumentation punctuation."

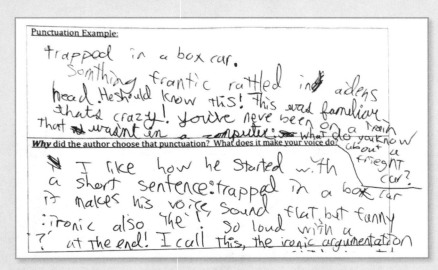

Teaching Point: Writers can use a mix of long and short sentences with varied punctuation to make a piece more interesting and create different feelings for a reader.

What Do Charlotte and Nathan's Conferences Have in Common?

Though each conference started out focusing on either reading or writing, the conversations were fluid, and went back and forth between the two subjects. It helped, of course, that the students were accustomed to this sort of discourse; all were in classes where the teacher took opportunities to make reading and writing connections whenever possible, planned or unplanned.

As different as the teaching points were for each student, both conferences followed a similar trajectory.

- First, the student spoke specifically about her or his book or piece of writing.
- I pushed them to think in terms of making a teaching point more transferable that references both reading and writing.
- We went back to the specific, relating the idea to that day's book or piece of writing.
- Next, we agreed on an assignment to practice and solidify the learning.
- Last, I reiterated how this idea connected reading and writing.

Practical Tips: Everyday Classroom Routines That Forge Reading and Writing Connections

When I was principal at New York City's P.S. 6, our professional development initiative one year was vocabulary instruction. Although we read Isabel Beck's research (2002) and tried out various programs, the teachers were not getting the results they wanted—with one exception.

For whatever reason, the children in Barbara Rosenblum's third-grade class were like little thesauruses. They marched through the halls discussing the "nuances" of school rules, felt the cafeteria's pizza was "lackluster," and appreciated the "idiosyncrasies" of the music teacher. How did those eight-year-olds develop such a multisyllabic lexicon? When I asked Barbara, she shrugged and invited me to come visit.

I spent the entire morning observing in her classroom, from arrival until lunchtime, and what I saw was startlingly simple. From the moment her kids walked in the door, Barbara lost no time, using "million-dollar words" whenever possible. She was "flummoxed" at a student forgetting his homework, and "ecstatic" over how well the class had done on yesterday's quiz. Whenever a student made an unusual word choice in a class discussion, she called attention to it and celebrated: "Did you hear that, boys and girls? Lashawn used the word 'extraordinary'!" By valuing interesting vocabulary and making it the norm in the room, students began to use sophisticated language routinely. It was, after all, just what you did in Ms. Rosenblum's class.

The same principle applies to reading and writing connections. Though there is certainly value in teaching explicit lessons about how the two overlap, the most powerful way to get students to think across these subjects is by modeling the idea in our daily discourse. Some of this may be planned for, but much of it— arguably the more impactful practice—comes from seizing opportunities to point out specific links whenever possible, throughout the day.

It is a mistake, though, to assume that those opportunities will arise solely by accident. As with any instruction, there are specific, concrete classroom rituals and routines we can establish to ensure reading and writing connections will come up on a regular basis. What follows are six effective ways to scaffold and support this important, not-so-subliminal message.

1. **Keep class read-alouds and mentor texts available when conferring in writing, for quick referral.** It is always best, whenever possible, to teach from texts students already know. Over the course of a year, most teachers build a large repertoire of familiar mentor texts from class read-alouds and various lessons. Many find it helpful to think ahead about which texts can be used to teach particular strategies and keep them close at hand during writing conferences for easy reference.

Professional Development/Grade-Meeting Activity: Have colleagues bring favorite read-alouds, articles, and texts to share. Together, brainstorm which writing techniques they can teach in conferences. For example, what books provide good examples of sensory description, punctuation, varied sentence length? Which articles demonstrate nonfiction text features, how to integrate quotes from experts, etc.?

---

2. **Have students keep their independent reading or book club book available during writing time, so when a new strategy is taught they can "check to see how the author did it."** It's one thing for a teacher to refer to a favorite mentor text in a conference. It's another for a student to begin using these texts on her own. Naturally, children will benefit from first seeing an adult go into a book to study a writing technique, but over time there's no reason this can't become a student-led inquiry. Some teachers ask students to keep their latest independent reading and/or book club book on their desk during writing time, and encourage them to "see if you can figure out how *your* author did it" when a teaching point comes up during an individual conference.

3. **Keep writing notebooks and drafts out during reading conferences, to make notes on an author's craft decisions.** During independent reading time, it is a good idea for students to have their writer's notebooks and/or current pieces readily available, along with some sticky notes. When conferences take a "reading like a writer" turn, they can jot down particular techniques that inspire them for future (or immediate!) use.

4. **Take a moment at the end of each day's read-aloud to point out an author's interesting craft move.** Most elementary and middle school teachers read to and with students throughout the day. One routine that encourages reading and writing connections is to pre-select a passage from each text that demonstrates an interesting craft move, and share it with students at the end of a read-aloud or lesson. "I try to do this every day, as often as possible," says Courtney Al Moreno. "It only takes a minute, and it ends up being infectious. Kids start coming up to me to share passages from their books, even at break times!"

5. **Combine reading and writing notebooks, rather than having one of each.** Some teachers find having students combine their reading and writing notebooks encourages natural connections between the two subjects. One way to organize such a setup is to have the reading section begin at the cover of the notebook, and start the writing entries from the back. Alternatively, a divider halfway through may be used to delineate the two sections.

6. **Plan "literacy workshop" days where individual students get to choose whether they want to work on reading or writing.** As Ellin Keene has suggested, one way to structure literacy instruction is a model where reading and writing are not treated as separate subjects—a "literacy studio" approach, where children can work on either or both in a single period. Some teachers prefer to have special designated days of the week where students have the option of working on one or the other. (Asking students to indicate on a class chart their subject for the day can help us stay on top of who is doing what when!) On those days, it makes sense, whenever possible, to teach mini-lessons that explicitly address reading-writing connections. Another way to reinforce these connections during independent work time is to give students the option of whether they want a conference in reading or writing.

SOME FINAL THOUGHTS

"The Hate You Give by Angie Thomas? I just want to put this out there, I like to write, I do not like to read…. So going into this book I was like, here we go, another book I'm not going to read. But for some reason—I mean for many reasons—I just kept reading it. There's just so much I could say about this, I'm stuttering! What happens in the book is something we can all relate to. It doesn't matter your skin color, it doesn't matter your gender, it doesn't matter your background. We can all relate to this because these events in this book have happened, we've all seen them, it's been all over the news, we've all been through it. I mean 2020, right? What I took away from this book is just how messed up this world is. It tells you. It explains."

—Paulina, eighth grader at the American Embassy School, New Delhi, India

In the introduction to this book, I suggested that when conferences become opportunities to find the spark in an individual child and focus on strengths—rather than on what she or he *can't* do—we move a little closer to equity.

I believe that. Passionately. It's what inspired me to write this book. But there is important work to be done in addition to conferences if we are to truly move forward.

During my writing process—2020, moving into 2021—all hell broke loose. Teachers around the world were struggling to figure out the on-again-off-again, virtual-to-hybrid-to-in-person whirlwind of how to do school during a global pandemic—all while trying to stay healthy and safe themselves, sometimes amid unspeakable personal loss. Breonna Taylor and George Floyd were murdered in cold blood by White policemen, shining a much-needed, painful light on the racism that pervades America. Hate crimes against Asian, Jewish, and Muslim people were reported almost daily throughout Europe and North America. The #MeToo movement was exposing sexism and misogyny around the globe.

It was impossible to be unchanged by all of this. A long-overdue reckoning was set in motion all over the world. At the same time, educators felt enormous pressure to combat the possibility of "learning loss" that might occur with so much interrupted instruction. The tension between covering curriculum and slowing down to recognize the social and emotional needs of the kids in front of us felt more stressful than ever.

When the normal order of things was thrown into disarray and dealing with individual kids' unique situations was an urgent priority, it became painfully clear that by sticking to a prescribed curriculum, which didn't acknowledge those realities, we ran the risk of alienating many of our precious learners.

Happily, most teachers I know around the world rose to the occasion. "It was awful having to stay calm and keep it together with all that was going on," Courtney Al Moreno, at the American Embassy School in New Delhi, India, reflected. "But out of necessity I ended up doing most of my teaching through individual conferences, and it felt like I got to know my students in ways I never had before."

So yes, if conferences are treated as opportunities to help children establish identities as readers and writers, we move a little closer to equity. But it also matters what else is going on in the classroom.

This is not a book about curriculum. But it is not a book *against* curriculum either. Rather, it is a plea for balance between the need for teaching specific content and the need to honor the spark in every student, of every background, in schools all over the world.

Clearly some curricula are better than others, and having end-year expectations doesn't mean it's impossible to be responsive to individual students. As Cornelius Minor bluntly puts it in his seminal book, *We Got This* (2019):

"What we choose to teach can do great harm to children if we are not careful. Harmful curriculum is any curriculum that:

- does not see students or the very specific lives they lead.
- is not flexible enough to be altered by the teachers who seek to use it.
- does not educate or grow the practitioner."

This is not a book about curriculum. But it is not a book against curriculum either. Rather, it is a plea for balance between the need for teaching specific content and the need to honor the spark in every student, of every background, in schools all over the world.

In most instructional settings—whole-class lessons, small-group work—we "backward map," thinking first about desired outcomes and planning the best way to get there, which makes sense when our aim is to cover specific content.

In a reading or writing conference, it's important to enter without a preconceived outcome in mind. Sometimes the teaching point will neatly dovetail or reinforce what we are covering in the planned curriculum, but often it can go in a different direction and address the passion, or interest, or singular identity of the child in front of us.

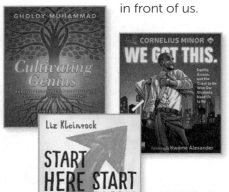

Still, for these sorts of individual reading and writing conferences to be effective, they must exist side-by-side with a culturally responsive, anti-racist curriculum that prioritizes, in the words of Dr. Gholdy Muhammad, "1) identity development, 2) skill development, 3) intellectual development, and 4) criticality." There are several important books out there that get into the details of planning such a curriculum. I especially recommend Dr. Muhammad's *Cultivating Genius* (2020); Cornelius Minor's *We Got This* (2019); and Liz Kleinrock's *Start Here, Start Now* (2021), among others. Those titles would be ideal companion texts to this one.

Along with a complementary curriculum, there are certain classroom conditions that I believe are critical to the success of reading and writing conferences. Here, in no particular order, are some thoughts about what we, as teachers, should keep in mind.

First, if we are to encourage student choice so children can pursue their own ideas and develop reading and writing identities, they need resources to choose *from*. This means providing a variety of texts that reflect who they are—and not just from a historical perspective. As African American children's author Jason Reynolds laments, reflecting on his experience in school, "It wasn't that the teachers were bad. From what I can remember, they were pretty good. It was about the selection of books. It was about not seeing my young life reflected back to me: my family dynamics, the noise and complexity of my neighborhood, the things I loved, like ice cream trucks and Kool-Aid."

Let's take a moment to unpack Reynolds's point. Many classrooms and schools, in a good-hearted effort to diversify their libraries, stock up on books about civil rights leaders, slavery, stories about immigration and oppression, etc. Clearly that is not a bad thing—but if those are the only books representing a culture, children won't connect to them, nor recognize their own present, day-to-day lives. (This isn't only an American problem; think of Zaima, the fourth-grade girl from Pakistan we met back in Chapter Three. She couldn't believe a book about a girl like her existed in the world, let alone right there in her classroom library in Hong Kong.)

As important as it is to ensure such representation, it isn't enough to *just* have books that reflect students' ethnicities and backgrounds and interests. Rudine Sims Bishop (1990) reminds us that in addition to mirrors, kids need windows into other experiences—especially ones that help them become more empathic to others. When middle schooler Ava (in Chapter Three) read *Never Fall Down*, she began to understand something about the human experience of being victimized by the Khmer Rouge—and experienced empathy for a life and situation far removed from her own experience.

Children are curious, always seeking to understand and weigh in on the world around them, whether it's close to home or not. "It's naive of adults to believe that young people aren't aware of what is going on in the world," reflects Jason Reynolds (2017). "The best thing we can do to confront that is to help them navigate it. We can help them say, 'These things are happening. What does that mean for your life?'" (Dawson, 2017) Having texts (and kind adults) available to help them figure it out can make an enormous difference. Paulina, the eighth grader quoted in this section's epigraph, is a Black African German girl going to school in India—but reading *The Hate You Give* helped crystallize her thinking about what she'd been hearing in the news way off in the United States. ("*It tells you. It explains.*")

The books we offer children are critically important in creating conditions that allow them to recognize, name, and extend their own lines of thinking, to be sure. But book selection on its own isn't enough. Teachers—especially White teachers working with students of color (I include myself)—need to do the work of examining their own assumptions and not projecting them onto students. My colleague, author and thinker Colleen Cruz, tells an illuminating story about an experience in an adult writing workshop:

> "I was writing about Mexican meatball soup, and it was a funny story. And the teacher sat down to confer with me and wanted me to write a sad story. She wanted me to get in touch with my Mexican American side, and she kept fighting with me that I needed to cry on the page. It was the

weirdest thing. At some point I realized it was because she had a vision of the story she wanted me to tell. She did not want a funny story about Mexican meatball soup. She ended up giving me a lower grade, and her comment was, "You just didn't dig deep enough." People come with their preconceptions, and they don't even know that's what they're doing. She couldn't see joy, she couldn't see humor, she wanted a sob story. So when I was writing about *my* identity, it didn't fit her vision of how that story should go."

This cautionary tale raises an important and uncomfortable issue. As a species, human beings inevitably make generalizations. Sometimes this works to our advantage, as when a doctor weighs factors such as weight, age, or whether someone is a smoker to calculate risk of disease. But as Malcolm Gladwell (2006) points out, "Another word for generalization...is 'stereotype,' and stereotypes are usually not considered desirable dimensions of our decision-making lives."

If as teachers we create conditions for the learners in our care to recognize and respect individual differences and perspectives, we have the potential to make a bigger impact than those in almost any other profession.

Teachers tend to be people who care deeply about children. I've never known one who would willingly do anything to harm or discourage a student. But if we are to work toward equity in schools—and ultimately in the larger world—it is essential for teachers to do the difficult work of examining their own preconceptions. This is true for any adult who works with children, but it is especially critical for teachers who come from positions of privilege and work with students from diverse backgrounds—in the United States and around the world. The White adult who criticized Colleen because she "didn't dig deep enough" in her writing no doubt thought she was being helpful—but in the end allowed her own ideas about what it meant to be Mexican American to get in the way of hearing the perspective of someone who actually *was*.

Confronting these difficult issues is a daunting prospect. It is easy to despair, to feel such problems are beyond the scope of one adult in a classroom. But, if as teachers we create conditions for the learners in our care to recognize and respect individual differences and perspectives, we have the potential to make a bigger impact than those in almost any other profession.

It all comes back to the radical idea of listening to children. If individual reading and writing conferences become a place where students learn to recognize, extend, and share their *own* unique perspectives, we help society move in the direction of equity—one child at a time.

REFERENCES

Allington, R., & Gabriel, R. (March 2012). "Every child, every day." *Educational Leadership*, Vol. 69, No. 6.

Anderson, C. (2019). *A teacher's guide to writing conferences.* Portsmouth, NH: Heinemann.

Bishop, R. S. (Summer 1990). "Mirrors, windows, and sliding glass doors." *Perspectives: Choosing and Using Books for the Classroom*, Vol. 6, No. 3.

Brison, T. (2020). "Neuroscience explains the astonishing benefits of reading like a writer—even if you don't plan on becoming one." cnbc.com

Calkins, L. (1994). *The art of teaching writing, new edition.* Portsmouth, NH: Heinemann.

Calkins, L., and colleagues. (2014). *Writing pathways: Performance assessments and learning progressions, grades K–8.* Portsmouth, NH: Heinemann.

Coulson, J. (2019). *10 things every parent needs to know.* New York: HarperCollins.

Cruz, M. C. (2020). *Risk. Fail. Rise: A teacher's guide to learning from mistakes.* Portsmouth, NH: Heinemann.

Culham, R. (2003). *6 + 1 traits of writing: The complete guide, grades 3 and up.* New York: Scholastic.

Dawson, M. (2017, October 21). How rap turned me into a successful poet. *The New York Post.* https://nypost.com/2017/10/21/how-rap-turned-me-into-a-successful-poet/

Duke, N. K., Pearson, P. D., Strachan, S. L., & Billman, A. K. (2011). Essential elements of fostering and teaching reading comprehension. In S. J. Samuels & A. E. Farstrup (Eds.), *What research has to say about reading instruction* (4th ed., pp. 51–93). Newark, DE: International Reading Association.

Emdin, C. (2016). *For white folks who teach in the hood...and the rest of y'all, too.* Boston: Beacon Press.

Feigelson, D. (2008). *Practical punctuation: Lessons in rule making and rule breaking, grades K–8.* Portsmouth, NH: Heinemann.

Feigelson, D. (2015). *Reading projects reimagined: Student-driven conferences to deepen critical thinking.* Portsmouth, NH: Heinemann.

Gladwell, M. (January 2006). "Troublemakers: What pit bulls can teach us about profiling." *The New Yorker.*

González, J., Barros-Loscertales, A., Pulvermüller, F., Meseguer, V., Sanjuán, A., Belloch, V., & Avila, C. (2006). "Reading cinnamon activates olfactory brain regions." *NeuroImage.*

Guthrie, J. T., & Humenick, N. M. (2004). Motivating students to read: Evidence for classroom practices that increase reading motivation and achievement. In P. McCardle & V. Chhabra (Eds.), *The voice of evidence in reading research* (pp. 329–354). Baltimore: Paul H. Brookes Publishing Co.

Iyer, P. (2014). *Times of India* interview.

Keene, E. O., & Zimmermann, S. (2007). *Mosaic of thought: The power of comprehension strategy instruction, second edition.* Portsmouth, NH: Heinemann.

Keene, E. O. (2012). *Talk about understanding: Rethinking classroom talk to enhance comprehension.* Portsmouth, NH: Heinemann.

Keene, E. O. (2018). *Engaging children: Igniting a drive for deeper learning.* Portsmouth, NH: Heinemann.

Kendi, I. X. (2019). *How to be an antiracist.* New York: One World.

Kleinrock, L. (2021). *Start here, start now: A guide to antibias and antiracist work in your school community.* Portsmouth, NH: Heinemann.

Krashen, S. (December 2011). "Academic proficiency (language and content) and the role of strategies." *TESOL Journal*, Vol. 2, Issue 4.

Marchetti, A., & O'Dell, R. (2021). *A teacher's guide to mentor texts.* Portsmouth, NH: Heinemann.

Minor, C. (2019). *We got this: Equity, access, and the quest to be who our students need us to be.* Portsmouth, NH: Heinemann.

Morrison, T. (2014). Interview with Rebecca Sutton, National Endowment for the Arts, *The art of failure: The importance of risk and experimentation*, No. 4.

Muhammad, G. (2020). *Cultivating genius: An equity framework for culturally and historically responsive literacy.* New York: Scholastic.

Myhill, D., Lines, H., & Jones, S. (2020). "Writing like a reader: Developing metalinguistic understanding to support reading-writing connections." pp. 107–122, *Reading-writing connections: Towards integrative literary science.* Berlin: Springer.

National Governors Association Center for Best Practices, Council of Chief State School Officers. (2010). *Common Core State Standards: Anchor standards for writing.* Washington D.C.

Noguera, P. (2016). Leadership Summit Speech, American Reading Company.

Paul, A. M. (March 17, 2012). "Your brain on fiction." *New York Times.*

Rousseau, J. J. (A. Bloom, Translator). (1762). *Emile, or on education.* New York: Perseus.

Saunders, G. (2021). *A swim in the pond in the rain: In which four Russians give a master class on writing, reading, and life.* New York: Random House.

Scardamalia, M., & Bereiter, C. (1987). Knowledge telling and knowledge transforming in written composition. In S. Rosenberg (Ed.), *Advances in applied psycholinguistics, vol. 1. Disorders of first-language development; vol. 2. Reading, writing, and language learning* (pp. 142–175). Cambridge University Press.

Shubitz, S. (2016). *Craft moves: Lesson sets for teaching writing with mentor texts.* Portland, ME: Stenhouse.

Vygotsky, L. S. (1978). *Mind in society: The development of higher psychological processes.* Cambridge, MA: Harvard University Press.

APPENDIX

All appendix items are also available at scholastic.com/RadicalListeningResources.

Content of Comprehension: A Cheat Sheet for Conferring

METACOGNITIVE STRATEGIES	TEXT-BASED CONTENT
What readers do in their heads	*What's on the page, not in readers' heads*

<table>
<tr>
<td>

- **Prioritize**
  Deciding what's more and less important.

- **Infer**
  Reading between the lines, understanding what the author is implying without saying directly.

- **Question and Argue With the Text**
  Not taking things at face value, e.g., noticing what information is left out of a news report, thinking a character action in a story is unrealistic.

- **Make Connections**
  Accessing prior knowledge; connecting to personal experiences, other books, and/or things we know about in the world.

- **Evoke Sensory and Emotional Images**
  Visualizing what's happening in a text; imagining what it sounds, feels, or tastes like; feeling the feelings of a character, or the mood of the story.

- **Monitor for Meaning**
  Knowing what to do when something in a text is confusing or complicated.

- **Synthesize**
  Connecting the dots, within or between texts, e.g., understanding how something on the first page connects to a detail on the second page, or how an idea in one book connects to another.

Adapted from *Mosaic of Thought* (Keene & Zimmerman, 2007)

</td>
<td valign="top">

- **Story Elements**
  Plot, character, setting, movement through time, problem/solution/reflection.

- **Literary Devices**
  Such as metaphor, simile, personification, alliteration, etc.

- **Punctuation**
  Such as exclamation marks, parentheses, em-dashes, question marks, etc.

- **Informational Text Features**
  Such as captions, subtitles, sidebars, italics, etc.

- **Informational Text Structures**
  How the text is written, such as problem/solution, cause/effect, question/answer, etc.

</td>
</tr>
</table>

Steps in a Reading Conference

1 **Start with a thinking question,** e.g., "What are you thinking about [name of text]?" *Don't* begin by asking for a retell. This may be useful for the teacher, but is not engaging for the student.

2 **Listen for the most interesting thing the reader says or does,** and jot down her specific words or phrases. (If the student defaults to a retell/summary, listen for something that sounds like an idea or opinion.)

3 **If possible, name the reader's line of thinking** in general, transferable language that could apply to other books as well—and ask her to reflect on it, e.g., "It seems what you are doing as a reader is…am I right?"

4 **Ask the student to find a part in the book** that illustrates what she is noticing or thinking about.

5 **Ask the reader to say more about that thing.** Listen for the most interesting part of the reader's response. Ask her to say more about *that*. (Ask some form of "Say more about that" at least three times before entering with your own content!)

ASSESS AND DECIDE

6 **Look and listen for a partial understanding.** Which comprehension strategy/strategies can you build on?

7 **Name the partial understanding in transferable language** that is about more than today's book, so it can be generalized as a strategy for future reading, e.g., "It seems like you are the type of reader who…."

TEACH

8 **State a teaching point** that extends the partial understanding, in language that can apply to the next book, and the book after that, e.g., "One important thing readers need to do is…"

9 **Negotiate concrete, specific work to do in today's text** to practice and extend the teaching point (e.g., sticky notes, reading notebook, graphic organizer). Have the students do a "try-it." Agree on how many, how long, due date, etc. for this assignment.

10 **Articulate the teaching point as a final comment, connecting it to future reading,** e.g., "Doing this work will help you practice…."

Qualities of Writing/Writing Cycle: A Cheat Sheet for Conferring

QUALITIES OF WRITING *What we teach when we teach writing, regardless of genre*	STAGES OF THE WRITING CYCLE *What we may teach at different points in the writing process*
Structure/Organization MACRO: • Transitions, i.e., how to get from one section of a piece to the next • Reordering sections of a piece • Story structure, e.g., where and how to introduce characters, problem, solution, etc. • Essay structure, e.g., thesis statement, examples, conclusion • Informational text *structure*, e.g., topic sentence, sequence and grouping of information • Informational text *features*, e.g., captions, subtitles, graphs, and charts MICRO: • Thinking about the sequence of sentences in a specific paragraph, e.g., varying sentence length, putting information in an appropriate order, etc. **Focus/Detail/Elaboration** • Which parts need additional sensory or descriptive detail • Which parts require additional info or explanation • Where to take out unnecessary detail • Deciding which sections should be longer or shorter **Craft/Voice** • "Talking to the reader," i.e., writing in a conversational tone • Combining action and description in the same sentence (e.g., "Her black dreadlocks bounced up and down as she ran toward the goal line") • Following a long, multi-clause sentence with a very short one, for emphasis • Showing (not telling) character emotion through facial expression and/or movement • Conveying a mood through setting description • Describing by comparing (e.g., metaphor/simile/personification) • Varying the signifying verb in dialogue, e.g., "she exclaimed" vs. "she said" **Conventions** • Dividing a sentence into clauses • Varying ending punctuation • Punctuating dialogue • Following a long clause with a short one • Using punctuation to create pauses	**Prewriting** • Planning out the sections of a piece with a graphic organizer (e.g., flow chart, timeline, outline) • Narrowing down a topic with a semantic web • Freewrite about your topic to generate content • Gather information about a nonfiction topic **Drafting** • Engaging lede • Rising action (narrative) • Reflective conclusion (essay, narrative) • Varying internal thinking/feeling and external action (narrative) • Expository text structures (e.g., question/answer, cause/effect, problem/solution, chronological) • Summative conclusion (expository) **Revising** • Almost anything in drafting can also be taught during revision • Reordering sections in a larger piece, or sentences in a specific section • Word choice: using more unique or descriptive vocabulary • Where to add dialogue, or sensory detail, or physical description • Taking out parts that seem redundant or too long • Mixing up long and short sentences to keep it interesting **Editing/Proofreading** • Checking for typos, spelling, punctuation, syntax, grammar mistakes • Checking for unnecessary repetition • Looking for places where sentences that are too long may be broken up into shorter ones • Looking for places where shorter sentences may be combined into longer, more complex ones

Steps in a Writing Conference

RESEARCH AND DISCOVER

1 **Start with a thinking question,** e.g., "What are you working on in today's writing?" If the student has difficulty explaining, ask what part she is working on.

2 **Scan the writing quickly to get an idea of the kind of work the student is doing.**

3 **Ask the student to describe or show a specific part** in her writing that shows what she is working on.

4 **Ask her to say more about that thing.** Ask more than once.

ASSESS AND DECIDE

5 **Look and listen for a partial understanding.** Which quality of writing can you build on?

6 **Prioritize a direction for teaching.** Use the student's partial understanding as a jumping-off point for teaching something new about writing (ZPD).

TEACH

7 **State a teaching point** that extends the partial understanding, in language that can apply to the next piece of writing, and the piece of writing after that. (Show an example in a mentor text, when possible.)

8 **Have the student apply the teaching point** to today's piece of writing (a "try it"). Negotiate parameters with the student, such as how many examples, where in the piece to try it, etc.

9 **Articulate the teaching point** as a final comment, connecting it to future writing, e.g., "Doing this work will help you practice…"

Reading Conference Note-Taking Form

Name	Book Title and Author	Strengths	Teaching Point	Project Description	Due Date

Reading Conference Tracking Sheet

Name:	Class:	Date:

Pre-Conference Notes	Conference Structure:
	• Listen • Ask reader to say more on selected topic/idea • Jot down notes • Name skill (teaching point) • Create assignment • Review teaching point

Text Title:

Conference Notes

Name Skill/Strategy (Teaching Point):

Assignment:

Due Date:

Next Steps:

Reading Conference Record-Keeping Form

Name:	Class:

Date:	Book:	Page:

What We Talked About	Strategy Taught by Teacher	What Students Will Work On

Date:	Book:	Page:

What We Talked About	Strategy Taught by Teacher	What Students Will Work On

Date:	Book:	Page:

What We Talked About	Strategy Taught by Teacher	What Students Will Work On

Reading Conference Reflection Sheet

Name:	Date:

Book Title:	Author:

In five or fewer sentences, summarize your book so far:

Add a photo of part of your conference assignment that shows your best thinking:

How did your conference assignment help you develop your thinking about *this* text?

Describe how this work might help you when you read other books:

Jesse Meyer, a teacher at the Hong Kong International School, devised this reflection sheet.

Writing Conference Note-Taking Form

Date:	Name:
	Compliment: **Teaching Point:** **Next Step:** **Quality/Qualities of Writing:**
	Compliment: **Teaching Point:** **Next Step:** **Quality/Qualities of Writing:**
	Compliment: **Teaching Point:** **Next Step:** **Quality/Qualities of Writing:**

INDEX